LEARN, LABOR, LOVE, LAUGH - LIVE

LEARN, LABOR, LOVE, LAUGH - LIVE

A FATHER'S DAILY THOUGHTS TO HIS SON

Dr. Paul F. MacVittie

ReadersMagnet, LLC

"The 4 L's in the book offer me a daily reminder to harmonize my life instead of balance it. They keep me focused on what is truly important, and help build a foundation for living and leading a mindful life."

-Jannell MacAulay, (Lt. Col. USAF - Ret.) PhD, Co-founder Warrior's Edge & TEDx Speaker

This book is dedicated to our incredible son, Mac, for whom each of these thoughts has been written.

–Dr. Paul F. MacVittie

Contents

Introduction

Farmers are a part of America's heritage. They know how to turn horse shit into fertilizer. Over the years, however, many people have forgotten how to emulate the wise farmer. The author of these "Thoughts," Paul MacVittie, spent many critical years of his youth not on a farm but in the concrete and brick jungle of an inner city. He grew up without the nurture or encouragement of positive family experience, yet has managed to find connectedness and purpose in his life. After the birth of his son, he provided this child with a home on a farm and, knowing that life is predicated upon the choices a person makes, he committed himself to teaching his son how to turn the "dung" experiences of life into assets. This is best learned when done consistently and in various circumstances, both expected and unexpected. This book is a collection of the kind of guidance and lessons that this father, Paul MacVittie, gave to his son, Mac, from before the time Mac entered the U.S. Air Force Academy through his becoming a pilot and eventually marrying and having a son of his own.

Dr. Paul F. MacVittie was born in 1937 in Buffalo, New York. When he was only eight months old, his parents were going through a divorce, and his father arranged for Paul to be kidnapped from his mother. There is no record of what happened to him for several years until he was dropped off by the kidnappers at a nunnery in Detroit, Michigan some 255 miles from home. Sometime later, he was reunited with his paternal grandparents in Buffalo, New York, where he lived until he was nine years old. Eventually, Paul's father and stepmother came to Buffalo and took Paul to live with them in Connecticut, but in the few years Paul had with them, he experienced no sense of connection of family love or support because of dysfunctional issues between his father and stepmother. He ended up living with various other families in the inner city of Bridgeport, Connecticut, and eventually found his sense of connection from playing sports; coaches and teammates became his surrogate family. The intensity of Paul's commitment to his teams earned him opportunities for scholarships to a prep school and college in New England. After graduate school, Paul went on to engage in various professional disciplines, all working with people, ranging from a college coach, inspirational speaker and teacher, business personnel executive, to a psychodynamic psychotherapist (in his words, a "shrink") —a life coach.

His son, William Sanford, "Mac," was born in 1983, and Paul made the choice to be for his son the kind of father he never had himself. Moving the family to farmland he owned in rural New Hampshire, Paul created an atmosphere of individual responsibility and family support. The title of the book comes from one of the rituals father and son shared on a daily basis. At the end of the day, they would sit down by the fireplace (in the winter) or on the deck (during summer evenings) or wherever, to share how they had "learned, labored, loved, and laughed" that day. Paul always encouraged Mac to discover and commit himself to something he would love to do and then find someone who was willing to pay him to do it. While feeding, protecting and cleaning up after the sheep on the farm, Mac ultimately dreamed of becoming a pilot, the calling he could love and commit himself to. As a senior in high school in 2001, Mac applied to the Air Force Academy the day after the terrorist attacks on the World Trade Center and the Pentagon on September 11th. In June of

2002, Mac entered the Academy, committing himself to a career of service to his nation.

Once Mac was no longer living at home, Paul started sending him daily "Thoughts for Today," or TFTs, encouraging him, mentoring him and maintaining their close father/son relationship.

Here is one of the TFTs that describes his intended purpose:

March 21, 2014

Son,

Why the Thoughts for Today for all these years? Well, there are several reasons. The obvious one is that home is not a house where one lives, but it is the relatedness in which one lives. This relatedness remains dynamic regardless of geography. The rituals of taking time to listen and to touch form a connection that is eternal. In a strategic sense, these TFTs keep up the touching and the listening, and this is, of course, what rituals are meant to do. In ancient times, every social occasion had its rituals, from the greeting, the interaction and the dining, to the farewells. Patterns are a part of life, and from these patterns we learn a great deal. As an example, prayer and special music at bedtime were a norm for you. When a young person knows that they are listened to and touched, there is communicated to that individual the awareness that they are valued and prized. The end result of this is that in adulthood they function, in all interpersonal areas, out of a surplus rather than a deficit. One of the main assets of having rituals is the energy and strength that can be gathered from them. Holding hands around the table during a prayer of thanks is a perfect example. My prayer is that the ritual of these TFTs, through these many years, have served in some way to underscore the relatedness we have and thus undergird the truth that wherever you are, you are at home with us, and we with you. This awareness certainly gives me an energy and a truck-load of gratitude which reinforce the purpose to keep on keeping on.

Love Always, Dad

In continuing to provide his son with a psychological and spiritual surplus, rather than a deficit, Paul MacVittie also offers us, his readers, valuable insights into how we can turn shit into fertilizer, as well as create rituals and meaning in our own lives. While we seek to learn, labor, love and laugh every day, this book falls into three Chapters focused on Learning, Laboring and Loving. You will find examples of Laughter throughout these pages.

LEARN

2001 - 2008

GRAND AND GLORIOUS TRADITION

Best Account
May 25, 2001

Dear Mac,

So many great people confront their destiny in a remarkable way. Milton, after suffering blindness, writes his greatest works, *Paradise Lost* and *Samson Agonistes*. Milton's poetry is an example of how tragedy can be formed by art into a thing of beauty. You see, my son, the Miltons, the Keatses, the Beethovens, the Omar Khayyams are not afraid of confronting the worst and, not being afraid, they are released to open up to all the possibilities of life. Euripides gave excellent advice: "Events will take their course; it is not good our being angry at them. He is happiest who wisely turns them to the best account." (Plutarch, 1898) It is invariably not the circumstances of life that determine how we live or what we accomplish. It is the inner man that decides what he can do with those circumstances. The bird of paradise drops doodoo on everyone. One can walk around with doodoo or one can turn doodoo into fertilizer and blossom much like the flowers of the field. It all begins with how we see ourselves and what we expect from ourselves. Don't be afraid of the doodoo. This day fashion your destiny, my son, and turn it "to your best account."

Love, Dad

Making a Better Place
April 14, 2002

Dear Mac,

I have been thinking about one of our conversations in which you said you were afraid that you might not succeed. My comment to you was, "fear is not a good motivator" in fact, it is an unhealthy motive for anything. The best motive of all is a combination of Thanksgiving and Service: gratitude to God for the life and love that we have received and a commitment to make our lives count in the sense of making the world a better place because we are in it. This may sound like arrogance or pride. "How can little old me make a difference?" The fact is, it is not arrogance but good, clear thinking. The motive for studying is not fear of flunking but a quest for knowledge; the motive for living a wholesome life is not fear of illness, but rather to be effective and strong as long as possible; the motive for being a loving person is not to receive love but to enrich and make people aware of the fact that they are of great worth! Fear is crippling. I urge you never to be afraid of failure but rather to simply be committed to doing your best. You will make mistakes (we all do); you will have disappointments (we all have); however, you will go on motivated by gratefulness and service. I believe you are a *present*, a *gift* from God—in large part because logic suggested you should never have been born.[1]

---

1 For medical reasons, his mother's pregnancy was considered "high risk."

As a consequence, I have made many decisions on what I thought was best for you. I must say that I have been rewarded tenfold for those decisions by the joy and pride you have given me. So my son, let me assure you that your special place upon this planet earth is going exceedingly well. You have already had a positive impact and I am sure that in the days ahead it will only continue to be magnified! Confidence in God, a desire to serve and gratitude for His blessings in your life will banish fear and turn normal anxiety into a powerful ally as you simply do your best to be His powerful instrument in the days that lie ahead.

Love and hugs, Dad

United States Air Force Academy

Mac and his father, Parents' Weekend 2002

Grand Coulee
August 13, 2002

Dear Mac,

A thought on how to deal with frustration, inasmuch as profanity is not encouraged at the Air Force Academy. Whenever something is disappointing or upsetting to me, especially on the golf course, rather than saying "Oh f———" or "Oh s———", I mumble "Grand Coulee," which of course is the biggest DAMN in the world! Just a simple thought for today.

Love, Dad

In Remembrance
September 11, 2002

Dear Mac,

There are events which freeze our souls as if we were in a time warp.

A few of us start with December 7, 1941 (Pearl Harbor); others are riveted on November 22, 1963 (President Kennedy Assassination). I was in grad school doing an internship in a mental institution when a patient went running through the hall saying the President was shot. "Another nut," was my reaction, only to learn that his craziness was incredibly true.

Now a new date has been added: September 11, 2001. This year on the anniversary of being attacked, a rolling requiem of choirs crossing one-time zone to another will send a message of love and lament. However, there is another emotion lingering—it is that of *rage*. Over and over we watch the towers burn and fall. *Vulnerability*—a word usually associated with individuals, instantly described our entire nation, our society, our way of life. 9/11 was not simply a terrorist attack—after all, there had been terrorist attacks before. Over the centuries only a state could attack another state. Only a state had the resources, communications, technologies and armies to mount an attack of this magnitude. What 9/11 demonstrated is that now a small number of people using the weapons of biogenetic pathogens, air transport, and 'dirty bombs' can exploit a society like ours. People motivated by hate, jealousy or a perverse religion which preaches "jihad," have introduced a new era of warfare. Many things will change before we will again have the peace we took for granted before September 11. Our rage is justified but we cannot live, conduct our affairs, listen to our children, or fulfill our obligations in a context of perpetual rage. Theologians, psychologists and philosophers alike all give testimony that life demands a 'vital balance.' That balance is summed up in three words: Faith, Hope and Love. We are confronted with the reality of *choice*. The choice is to make this day count on every level. The stock traders, secretaries, investors, salespeople, and security forces working in the World Trade Center had no idea that 9/11 would be their last day on earth. Tragically it was. Vulnerability can cause us to live in fear or motivate us to reach out and live more abundantly than ever before. Hopefully this is the choice we will make, for this is the best way to remember 9/11.

Love, Dad

Resilience
October 6, 2002

Dear Mac,

Regarding your comment about being one of the top students at Brooks School and feeling just average or below average at the Academy, I know this won't make you feel any better but it should: from everything I hear and read about the Academy, it seems that the majority of cadets have at one time or another been on AP [academic probation.] As you have told me in the past and have learned, "What doesn't kill you makes you stronger." When you wrote the Academy in the essay part of your application, you said that one of the qualities that you learned from growing up on the farm that you most admired was *resilience*. I believe you have resilience and I believe, like it says in Philippians 4:13, that "you can do all things through Christ who strengthens you," even if temporarily you are on AP.[2] Rest assured that this in no way reduces my admiration and pride in who you are and who you are becoming.

Love, Dad

---

2   Two years later, in his Two Degree (junior) year at the Air Force Academy, Mac was made the squadron Academic NCO (noncommissioned officer) in charge of those fellow cadets in his squadron (dorm) who were on AP (academic probation). Given that authority, he implemented several positive motivational strategies that were so effective that the Academy put those strategies in place for a fourth of the entire Academy, for which he was recognized and honored in a full campus-wide ceremony.

Dealing with Dark Days
October 29, 2002

Dear Mac,

You are going to be entering into the dog-days of being a fourth class cadet. The weather is going to be harsh, academics are going to be as harsh if not harsher and that sneaky sense of being overwhelmed will probably become more pronounced. To be forewarned gives you the opportunity to be prepared. There are several things I want you to do:

(1)   I want you to pray every day. You don't have to pray just at night or just in the morning. Every time you put your hand in your pocket and feel that keychain with the words from Isaiah,[3] you can offer up a prayer, a prayer for guidance, a prayer for strength, a prayer for understanding and a prayer for peace, inner peace.

(2)   As well as praying every day, I want you to take advantage of the professors' willingness to give extra help and guidance. Also, look into whether there are any study groups. My guess is that, depending upon your schedule, seeking one-on-ones with the profs is the best source because you are not only getting information but encouragement.

---

3   Isaiah 40:31: "They who wait upon the LORD shall renew their strength, they shall mount up with wings like eagles, they shall run and not be weary, they shall walk and not faint."

(3)   One of your greatest qualities is your resilience, learned I am sure from all the times I dumped buckets of snow on you when you were seven or eight years old. In fact, I have a picture of me in the tractor dumping snow on you. Remember James Corbett, the famous boxer whose motto was, "One more round"? He said he fought bigger, stronger, faster opponents than he but he never fought an opponent that he couldn't outlast, and he became the heavyweight boxing champion of the world. "One more round" is the epitome of somebody who has no quit in them. You are like this, my son. You are tenacious, doggedly determined and motivated from the tip of your toes. You have what I have told you before is an incredible amount of *pluck*. You represent what is best about America.

I love you. Dad

Gyroscope
January 11, 2003

Dear Mac,

In the Old Testament, one of my favorite verses is "They that wait upon the Lord shall renew their strength; they shall mount up with wings as eagles."[4] Maybe we should change that to "mount up with wings as Falcons" [the mascot and name of the Air Force Academy sports team]. Anyway, it is the "waiting on the Lord" bit that I want to give as your thought for the day. I think what it actually means is taking time each day to be centered, the importance of which cannot be overstated. It enables a person not to react to circumstances as a ping-pong ball reacting to a paddle but rather like a gyroscope that is always in balance regardless of what is happening around it. Some people get centered through meditation, others by listening to music or by physically working out. I think the easiest way is by focusing. What you focus on, in nature or scripture for example, enables you to handle any situation and to do so from the perspective of an optimist. Optimism is not the result of wishful thinking but rather the result of being centered.

Love, Dad

---

4   Isaiah 40:31

Churchill and the Human Spirit
January 13, 2003

Dear Mac,

I was reading a biography of Winston Churchill last evening and they quoted one of his speeches in which he said, "Very few wars have been won by mere numbers alone. Quality, will power, geographical advantage, natural and financial resources, the command of the sea, and, above all, a cause which rouses the spontaneous surging of the human spirit in millions of hearts, these have proved to be the decisive factors in the human story." (Churchill, 1940) The accomplishments of great men throughout history, my son, have been accomplishments that were motivated and sustained by passions of the heart, whether it was a Pasteur looking for a way to stop disease or a Livingston exploring the dark continent of Africa or Lewis and Clark with the small valiant band crossing the Northwest Passage from Missouri to the Pacific, all of these followed the song in their heart and it got them through their own dark days. You too, have a passion in your heart to serve this great country of ours and I am convinced that with the challenges that now encumber you, you will be victorious. Churchill concluded his speech with a confidence that "the day will come when the joy bells will ring . . . when victorious nations, masters not only of their foes, but of themselves, will plan and build in tradition and in freedom a house of many mansions where there will be room for all." I am convinced that the academic, physical and military demands that challenge you at this time will cause you to gain a strength in all of these areas that will serve you and others in the decades that lie ahead.

Love, Dad

Optimum

February 14, 2003

Dear Mac,

The Latin word for 'best' is *optimum*, or, optimism in the face of difficulty. Human potential is always at its best in the face of challenge. Optimism is not something you can seek. It is a result of decision-making. One of the neat things I have learned in observing human behavior is that a person is not determined by conditions but is ultimately self-determining. In other words, we don't simply exist but always determine by our choices what our existence shall be! We cannot always change the world for the better but we can always change ourselves for the better, if necessary. I've concluded that what comes out of the heart depends on decisions, not on conditions. One of the things that has impressed me about you is the fact that you have personified this principle. That is why, on this Valentine's Day, I'm so thankful for your love. Your destiny is a result of decisions you have made with the various conditions and circumstances in which you have found yourself.

Love, Dad

Freedom Underlies Valuing
March 8, 2003

Dear Mac,

❝ Freedom is thus more than a value itself: it underlies the possibility of valuing; it is basic to our capacity to value." (May, 1981) So wrote Rollo May, and I agree with him. All values derive their value from being free. For instance, love: what value is love if not freely given? What value is courage if not manifested by choice? What value is honor if not freely embraced? Even philosophers, as illustrated by Schelling, proclaim, "The beginning and end of all philosophy is freedom." (Schelling, 1809) Rousseau confessed that he was overwhelmed by the "marvels done by free people to guard themselves against oppressors." (May, 1981) When I first saw you in your uniform at Parents' Weekend, we embraced and I said to you, "You have become a part of a grand and glorious tradition." It is a tradition commited to the freedom of which I have been writing. You have freely chosen this service. How proud I am of you!

Love, Dad

The Whole Course
April 8, 2003

Dear Mac,

Everyone who comes into your life has the capacity to be valuable. Emerson put it this way: "The whole course of things goes to teach us faith." (Emerson & Ed. Atkinson, 1940) *The Whole Course*—this means everything that comes your way, sort of like the Clint Eastwood film title, *The Good, the Bad and the Ugly* (Leone, 1966). As the Good Book teaches us, "God works in mysterious ways."[5] I grew up without a mother or a father. As a result, many scary things happened to me, so I chose to make sure I would be the best father I could be. Far from perfect, as you know, but determined to be what I never had. When I felt inadequate in terms of academics, I learned that Faith meant to use your mind as well as your heart, so God in His grace allowed me to be at the top of my class in grad school. I know from experience that what Emerson wrote is true. "The whole course of things goes to teach us faith."

Love, Dad

---

5   This common maxim comes from a quoted poem and hymn by William Cowper, "God works in a mysterious way."

Smile at the Task

April 11, 2003

Dear Mac,

Today's TFT comes fresh out of an incredible experience I
had today. I had been invited to play in a golf tournament
at a lovely golf course down here in Florida and was under the
impression that it started between 12:30 and 1:00 PM. As I was
sitting down with a cup of coffee at 8:10 AM, about ready to write
you a TFT, the phone rang and it was my host asking me where I
was because the tournament was about to start in twenty minutes.
He said that he would start without me and to get there ASAP.
He also called me a name which was not too affirming but, under
the circumstances, understandable. With great assistance from
your mother, within six minutes I was speeding down the road.
The ten-year-old car that I was driving had never been driven
like it was this morning. Now, this club that I was playing at is
thirty-five to forty minutes away under normal circumstances and
all I could do while driving was to laugh. I was laughing at the
fact that the name which my host had called me on the phone was
most appropriate. To make a long story short, I made it in record
time, was met at the Security Gate, driven to the third tee and,
without my shoes being laced, up hit my three iron into a sand
trap 190 yards away (a par three). From there, I proceeded to go
par, birdie, birdie, and all of a sudden my partner was calling me
sweet nothings. I learned something on the golf course that I had
never known before. If I am smiling as I address the ball, there
is not a tense muscle in my body and my focus is actually very

good. So, the word for the day is, take your task seriously and at the same time, smile. You will perform the task better. Oh, by the way, we came in second in the overall tournament with a bunch of neat prizes. And my host invited me to play with him next year!

Love, Your Smiling Dad

Exertions of Better Men
April 26, 2003

Dear Mac,

I know you had to feel great when on parade to honor the sponsors.[6] You really looked wonderful along with your squadron in your new uniforms. For me to see so many young men and women who stand out was reassuring. From reading the *New York Times*, I sense there is a generation prepared for accomodation, appeasement and surrender. I prefer the words of John Stuart Mill to *The Times*. He said, "War is an ugly thing, but not the ugliest of things. The decayed and degraded state of a moral and patriotic feeling, which thinks that nothing is worth war, is much worse. A man who has nothing for which he is willing to fight, nothing he cares about more than his own safety, is a miserable creature who has no chance of being free, unless made and kept so by the exertions of better men than himself." (Mill, 1862) You and your classmates are the better men!

Love, Dad

---

6   Each cadet was assigned a volunteer faculty or civilian 'sponsor,' into whose home the cadet was welcomed. The sponsor's home became an off-campus place of retreat from Academy rigors and duties. At this Founder's Day parade, these cadet sponsors were invited, along with other civic leaders, members of Congress, and parents of cadets.

Event versus Process
May 9, 2003

Dear Mac,

One of the things I have noticed about people, and culture in general, is that a great number of individuals are Event-oriented, not Process-oriented. Let me explain what I mean. A person may dream about the great position in the company with financial benefits and perks but often doesn't recognize the twelve-hour days or longer which it takes to get to that position. Or they are interested in hitting the ball longer and straighter but won't invest in the Process of learning good swing mechanics. Usually, special Events require a commitment to a Process. I think of the F-16s that flew over the Academy a couple of weeks ago, all eight of them in formation. Quite an Event! And as you are learning now at the Academy, quite a Process to get there. If you can keep your mind on the finish line, even the Process can be exhilarating. Have a great day.

Love, Dad

Importance of Thoughts
May 23, 2003

Dear Mac,

Y ou have come through this year with a great deal of accomplishment. I know it has been demanding, and at times, painful and scary.[7] Life is scary and painful at times. In the western world, we often misrepresent God's plan for us and expect life to be comfortable and free from challenges (problems). But nowhere, in any religious thought I have studied, are we guaranteed a pain-free life. Spiritual teachers have always shown there is an opportunity to grow through painful experiences and in doing so transcend or reach heights we wouldn't have without them. The way we think through these experiences releases an energy into our system. For example, a loving thought can relax our entire body; other thoughts are like a bomb going off, causing a reaction in our body that is negative (stomach tightens, etc.). All of this is to point out how important your thoughts are when facing challenge or unpleasant circumstances. The Apostle Paul spoke

---

7   The cadets during the first year at the Academy are called "doolies" (from the Greek word doúlos, meaning 'slaves'). From the time they enter the Academy in June through the following March, the students are put through rigorous basic-training type of challenges designed to push them beyond their self-imposed limits, psychologically, physically, and academically.

of being able to "do all things through Christ who strengthened him."[8] Quite a thought! Have a thoughtful day!

Love, Dad

---

8 Philippians 4:13

Excellence
August 9, 2003

Dear Mac,

As has been said, "The Society that scorns excellence in plumbing because plumbing is a humble activity—and tolerates shoddiness in philosophy because philosophy is an exalted activity, will have neither good plumbing nor good philosophy. Neither its pipes nor its theories will hold water." (Gardner, 1961) One of the great aspects of a good education is that you will not be leaky in your thinking. Your cognitive skills are being strengthened, as are the muscles in your body. The result of all of this will be a stronger community because you are a part of it.

Love, Dad

Freedom to Choose
September 3, 2003

Dear Mac,

*F*reedom is not something we have; freedom is what we are. This is what Viktor Frankl concluded in his concentration camp experience. No man can have his freedom wrest from him for he is always capable of choosing his attitude up to his last breath. Therefore, he can choose to rise above cultural or environmental destiny. Man retains the freedom and the possibility of deciding for or against the influence of his surroundings.[9] He may seldom exert this freedom or utilize this opportunity to choose; yet it is always open to him.

Love, Dad

---

9   The author often quotes Frankl, with whom he spent a weekend in California. Frankl's concepts of Logotherapy are an underpinning of the author's psychotherapeutic technique. Logotherapy contends that man's basic need in life is not pleasure or power but purpose/meaning.

Hammer and Anvil
September 5, 2003

Dear Mac,

The times the times we get pissed on or the times we work our ass off and it appears that no one cares—these are the things which should never be subtracted from our lives because these are the things which serve as a hammer. How we choose to deal with these blows shape us much like a blacksmith and his anvil. It is never the blows but the choices we make in relation to these experiences that determine our destiny. You have made some wonderful choices in your twenty years and I am confident you will continue to do so.

Love, Dad

Learning to Fall

September 17, 2003

Dear Mac,

There is a Spanish proverb that says, "He who would ride a horse must learn to fall." Of course, when everything goes right, it's blissful riding horses, flying airplanes, mountain climbing— whatever. Dealing with perfection isn't the challenge. How we deal with the *falls* we encounter is really what it's all about! Perhaps the greatest illustration I know that underscores this point was Thomas Edison. When asked how he dealt with thousands of his failed experiments, he simply replied, "I've never made a mistake. I've only learned from experience." (Edison, n.d.) Mac, you have demonstrated that you have the right stuff. You have *learned to fall* and, most importantly, gotten right back up on that horse again and ridden to victory! Keep up the good work.[10]

Love, Dad

---

10   Mac failed a GR (graded review—how the Academy refers to exams) in sophomore (Three Degree) chemistry that semester and was placed on academic probation at mid-terms. That meant he was restricted to base and could not leave campus. However, with proper motivation and mindset, he sought out extra instruction (tutoring) from another chemistry professor and passed the class by the end of the term.

Self-Talk
September 18, 2003

Dear Mac,

Most people I enjoy (like you) are polite, civil and affirming of others. Yet, I have observed that civility and politeness goes out of the proverbial window when they are talking to themselves. Self-talk is a dialogue that often takes place on the golf course: "What a jerk!" "I'm an asshole" "I can't putt worth anything." They wouldn't think of talking to anybody else this way but they continually do this demeaning chatter to themselves. The key to self-talk is reframing it to the positive by not seeing oneself as the scumbag who hit the awful shot, or the student who is stupid because he didn't do well on a test, but rather as the person who can come back or the student who will ace the next exam, etc., etc. So today, talk well to yourself. It makes all the difference in the world. You really deserve to be spoken kindly to because you are a great man.

Love, Dad

Dining with Demons

October 22, 2003

Dear Mac,

One of the phrases I use with patients is to "dine with the demon." It comes from my childhood experiences of the 'Boogie Man' or the 'Ragman'—scary people of my imagination who would overpower me or do something awful! When one opens the door to the "cellar" and turns on the light, the "boogie man" miraculously disappears for, in fact, he was never really there. And this is how I came up with the concept of "dining with the demons." I realized that one gains strength, courage and confidence when, in experience, you look fear in the face. Doing the thing we think we cannot do is one of the keys to a remarkable life. Have a Liberating Day.

Love, Dad

Unique
October 31, 2003

Dear Mac,

D avid Riesman may have said, "The idea that men are created free and equal is both true and misleading. Men are created different. They lose their social freedom and their individual autonomy in seeking to become like each other." (Riesman, 2000) The way I say it is, "We are all born originals, but many choose to die carbon copies." What a way to frustrate destiny. I thank God you are maintaining your unique and wonder-filled ways.

Love, Dad

Heart of Volunteer
February 9, 2004

Dear Mac,

Y ou have told me that Lt. Col. Doolittle, of Doolittle Hall on the campus of the USAFA, once said that there is nothing as strong as the heart of a volunteer. You are a volunteer. We don't have conscription in the United States. You have volunteered to join the Air Force. You have volunteered to go the most taxing route possible in the Air Force, namely the Air Force Academy. You, in essence, have volunteered to take upon yourself a discipline that is mental, physical and spiritual—not for a few weeks or months but minimally for a decade. There will be days during this period when responsibility will seem laborious, demanding and at times boring. It is during these times that it is important that you remember why you volunteered—and that is to serve and, in serving, protect the values of the greatest nation in the history of the world—a nation which is made up of men and women of various backgrounds, talents, convictions and interests. It is a nation of people with strengths and weaknesses and it is precisely because of this combination that your volunteering is so precious. There are at this very moment people who would seek to destroy this nation and its values for reasons that transcend understanding. When you awaken each morning for the task at hand, I want you to remember that everything you do, from the academics to the military to the physical fitness tests and demands, that it is for the most noble cause there is. You are part of a grand and noble tradition, and you not only have my gratitude and profound admiration but also are the source of a fatherly pride that is immeasurable. Have a great day.

Love, Dad

Clarity of Mind
April 8, 2004

Dear Mac,

There are a lot of principles in life, or basics as we say in golf or any athletic endeavor such as grip, stance, posture etc. One of the basics in life is the perception principle. For example, what you see is what you get. This all begins in the area of the mind. When a person is defeated in his mind, or is overwhelmed by self-defeating thoughts, he or she needs a mind overhaul. What I have observed is that most people who mess up their lives are messed up in their thinking. You may recall a book that Norman Vincent Peale sent to me with some very kind words inscribed therein. The title of the book is *You Can If You Think You Can.*[11] Therefore it comes as no surprise that two thousand years ago the Apostle Paul said to the people of Rome, "Be transformed [*or changed*] by the renewing of your mind."[12] I am not talking about mind games but mind clarity. Today, remember, "You can if you think you can." (Peale, 1974)

Love, Dad

---

11   The author was able, through persistence in the face of repeated denial, to arrange a meeting with Norman Vincent Peale. The inscription was "To Paul MacVittie who exemplifies the principles in this book, Norman Vincent Peale."

12   Romans 12:3

Being Yourself
September 15, 2004

Dear Mac,

One of my heroes whose thinking has influenced me significantly was Viktor Frankl. I spent a weekend with him thirty-five years ago with one other person (a psychology professor of mine). Anyway, this is something Frankl said: "Being human is being responsible. Man is a 'deciding being.' Man has a unique destiny that will not recur—no one else can do what a particular person can do. Everyone is unique and singular. Too many people do not recognize this and therefore abdicate their uniqueness through compromising themselves." (Frankl, 1986) Have a great day by being yourself.

Love, Dad

Americanism
September 30, 2004

Mac,

Teddy Roosevelt said, "Americanism means the virtue of courage, honor, justice, truth, sincerity, and hardihood—the virtues that made America. The things that will destroy America are prosperity-at-any-price, peace-at-any-price, safety first instead of duty first, the love of soft living, and the get-rich-quick theory of life." (Roosevelt, 1917) This was written in 1917 in a letter that Roosevelt sent to a meeting dealing with *Constructive Patriotism*. The qualities emphasized at the Air Force Academy seem to be taken right out of the heart of this man. These were ingrained in you before the Academy by shoveling sheep shit, putting up hay and bringing in firewood. You are the best.

Love you, Dad

Bonus from God

December 16, 2004

Dear Mac,

By-products are cool. They are like a bonus from God. I believe it was Ralph Waldo Emerson who once said that *it is one of the most beautiful compensations of this life that no man can sincerely try to help another without helping himself.* One of the reasons you have been recognized in this way[13] is that you didn't seek recognition—you just did your job. And look what happened.

Love, Dad

---

13   Mac was honored at the awards ceremony for his work as squadron Academic NCO. See the note for "Resilience," the TFT for October 6, 2002 (page 10).

Human Choice
February 14, 2005

Mac,

A patient once told me that she was not a human being until I had made her one. Don't get it wrong—I'm not in the God business. What she meant was that until she started seeing me, she saw herself as the helpless victim of circumstances. The empowerment I was able to give her was that dignity of choice. It was the enabling mechanism which allowed her to transcend the pitiable situation she was in. Choice led her to a sense of dignity and, as a result, from a closed heart to one that was open and alive—thus a human being!

Love, Dad

Believing in Yourself
April 18, 2005

Dear Mac,

The TFT comes from one of my favorites, the pioneering American Psychologist William James, who realized a long time ago that people tend to become what they think of themselves. If you are going to get better at anything, whether it is being in shape physically, mentally or spiritually, you must first think of yourself as capable of doing so. One of the most important things to believe in is yourself. No matter how much someone else believes in you, it is more important that you believe in yourself. Remember the story that your mother used to read to you when you were young which involved the little red engine that went from "I think I can, I think I can" (Piper, 2005) to "I know I can!" Today, be like that little red engine.

Love, Dad

Significant Experiences

April 27, 2005

Mac,

The most significant experiences that transform lives often cannot be explained in human terms. They often transcend our reasoning and measuring abilities. They are so real they cannot be reduced to words. This is true of joy and sorrow, pleasure and pain. It may only be said of these experiences that they are *known*. You have had some of these experiences in your life as well as I, and countless others. I rest in these matters with the words of Scripture which state, "For we know that all things fit into a pattern for good according to His plan."[14] For myself, I could never understand why I should grow up without a mother or father, but now I know, in retrospect, it made me committed to being the best father I could ever be, and to always be there for you.[15] It was Kierkegaard who said, "Life can only be understood backward, but must be lived forward." (Kierkegaard, n.d.)

Love, Dad

---

14   Romans 8:28, as paraphrased by the author.

15   When the author was eight months old, he was kidnapped. Several years later he was left, under his legal name, at a Catholic convent in another part of the country. Eventually, he was returned to his paternal grandparents in Buffalo, New York, where he grew up with some of his aunts and uncles (his father was the eldest of thirteen children) until he was nine years of age.

Being versus Doing
May 8, 2005

Mac,

How I rejoice in the Air Force granting you your first choice of pilot classification. Make no mistake however about my feelings! Pilot, navigator, intelligence officer, whatever, *you* are the *man*! As I said yesterday, my joy runs over for you because it has been your desire; however, my pride in you is not based on what you do, but on who *you are*. So many people I have come to know in my lifetime have a Functional Identity or sense of self. It is a fragile existence. If they stop doing what they have been doing, they don't know who they are, and don't feel as if they matter. One doesn't matter because of their particular job; they matter because of who they have become. Regardless of your career path, my great pride in you is due to the man you have become. Your days ahead will be filled with a centeredness because of this. Now anticipate soaring and reaching out and "touching the face of God." (Magee, circa 1941)

Love, Dad

Psychosclerosis
May 23, 2005

Mac,

Here is a thought for you. Arteriosclerosis is a disease of hardening of the arteries or of the tissue. I have seen people in my practice who have what I would call *psychosclerosis*—a loss of flexibility of attitude or spirit. They don't know how to lighten up. I think the latter is more dangerous to health than the former. Just the doc in me reflecting on one of the things that life has taught me. I don't worry about you having either of these conditions.

Love, Dad

Anxiety
May 24, 2005

Mac,

Yesterday I had a visitor who was speaking about his anxieties. I related to him that there are two kinds of anxieties: healthy and unhealthy. Healthy anxiety makes you look both ways when crossing a busy street; unhealthy anxiety causes you never to cross the street. Kierkegaard felt that anxiety can root out the mundane from a person's heart. I think he meant anxiety can clarify a person's values; for example, a near-death experience makes the song of the birds at 4:30 in the morning sound like a symphony rather than a damn nuisance. The reverse is also true: much anxiety is relieved by the clarifying of one's values. This is the context of Jesus' teaching in Matthew when he said, "Seek first the kingdom of God and His righteousness and all these things will be added to you."[16] So my son, your clear cut values will serve you well when it comes to removing unhealthy anxiety.

Love, Dad

---

16   Matthew 6:33

Laughter
May 26, 2005

Mac,

I was reading about a Russian human rights activist who was imprisoned. The guards would talk to him about the firing squad relentlessly. To overcome his fears he started making jokes about them being poor shots! Sharansky managed to overcome his fears with humor. He took an intolerable situation and joked about it. Take, for example, the 18th century philosopher Moses Mendelssohn. While walking down the street he accidentally bumped into a stout Prussian officer. "Swine!" bellowed the officer. Knowing if he returned the insult, physical abuse could follow, he took a different tack. He tipped his hat, gave the officer a courteous bow and replied, "Mendelssohn." (Sherman, 1992) It is amazing how often humor can turn any situation around. I have often used humor when facing the many surgeries I have undergone. I tell people when they think they are at the end of their rope, tie a knot, hang on and turn it into a swing! Remember how I brainwashed you into the four L's = Love, Learn, Labor, and LAUGH daily. It has served you exceedingly well and I am confident it will continue to do so in the future.

Love, Dad

Success Doing Your Best

June 27, 2005

Mac,

You are a success, and not because you have made the academic honor roll or the Commandant's honor roll, not because you have done excellently with your various leadership roles. You are a success *not because of results* you have known but rather because you have always done your *best*. This is why, as you start your "introduction to flight" today, you will continue to be a success—you have made a habit of simply doing your best! As Shakespeare says: "There is a divinity that shapes our ends, rough hew them how we will—" (Shakespeare, Hamlet (Act 5, Scene ii), 1992) You don't need to worry about the rough edges—they don't exist. Simply continue the habit of doing your best and that same divinity of which Shakespeare was writing will continue to shape your ends.

Love, Dad

Quilting
August 16, 2005

Mac,

There is something within each of us like the Creator (of course with a small c!). We are responsible for the degree we utilize the raw material at our disposal. This includes the experiences we encounter along life's journey. The craftsmen's fair was just held at Mount Sunapee and it dawned on me that a pretty good metaphor for life is a quilt. Now I'm no quilt maker, but what these people do with random pieces of material is remarkable and beautiful! The finished product is a joy to behold! Sometimes it seems that our experiences in life are just random stuff—a person here or there, a disappointment, a chance meeting, a conversation, a dinner engagement, whatever—but when we take time to reflect, and as the Good Book says "Give thanks in all things,"[17] we are well on our way to making a beautiful quilt out of everyday stuff. You my son are well on your way. Happy quilting.

Love, Dad

---

17   1 Thessalonians 5:18

Give Thanks
September 28, 2005

Mac,

These have not been ordinary days—we had to put Ski[18] out of his pain and discomfort; our house was struck by lightning and received significant damage from the subsequent fire, with repairs ongoing. The thought that comes to mind is the Scripture passage which teaches us "in all things give thanks."[19] The Apostle Paul is always talking about being thankful. Now, for a Jew who was very familiar with a whole boatload of doodoo, this is rather impressive, so in this sense it is good for me. I'm thankful for fourteen years of laughter and entertainment and companionship that "Ski Doodle" brought to our home; I'm thankful for talented craftsmen, such as the carpenters, electricians, painters and heating specialists who responded to repair our damaged home. I'm thankful for the expressions of concerns and willing spirits to diminish any discomfort we may have had during this time. I'm thankful that neither your mother nor I were harmed during the lightning and fire episode. The list of things for which to be grateful is quite long. It was easy to pick this verse from Scripture: "In all things give thanks." During this time, I'm especially grateful for you.

Love, Dad

---

18   This is a nickname for "Tchaikovsky," one of the family dogs.
19   1 Thessalonians 5:18

Concerning Exams

September 29, 2005

Mac,

Anxiety can be good. According to Kierkegaard, it roots out the mundane and the trivial in our lives. Thus, to be robbed of all anxiety, we would lose a constructive stimulant for life and survival. When our house was on fire, one might say there was sufficient stimulus to do important things! What clear values do is to set you free from paralyzing anxiety so one does not become frozen in place. I believe that faith thaws a person so they are not frozen by the vicissitudes of life. You, my son, have faith and I don't worry about you freezing to death.

Love, Dad

Prayer of St. Francis

October 8, 2005

Mac,

O ne of my favorite hymns is from the Prayer of St. Francis—
"Lord, Make me an Instrument of Thy Peace." At times
I am aware of screwing up that prayer and getting out of whack
with what really matters. At those times both music and nature
help me to return to harmony. A walk in the woods, gazing at
the stars on a clear night, breathing in the cool mountain air, all
of this gives me a feeling of being swept up into the arms of God
and renews the prayer of being His instrument. All self-reproach,
disappointment and guilt, which takes away from that peace, is
replaced with silence and harmony. You may not know some of
these struggles, but if and when you do, a walk in the woods, a
return to nature, literally opens a whole set of spiritual insights
and the accompanying blessings for you and through you.

Love, Dad

Pygmalion Experiment
October 20, 2005

Mac,

During the 70's a study was done with students. Teachers were given the names of the students who were projected to do well; other names were given of students who were projected to have difficulty. At the end of the year, the first group did very well and showed marked improvement. The other students showed very little improvement. What the teachers did not know was that the names which comprised the lists were randomly chosen. The experiment became known as "Pygmalion in the classroom." (Rosenthal, 1968) The name was taken from George Bernard Shaw's *Pygmalion*, which was the basis on which the musical "My Fair Lady" was written. We now know that people who expect to do well in areas of their lives do—and people who expect to do poorly in certain areas usually fail. Today, my son, have Great Expectations for yourself. Our Creator certainly has high expectations for you.

Love, Dad

Convictions

November 30, 2005

Mac,

Wherever the journey takes you, the companionship of clear convictions vanquishes loneliness. I thought of this while remembering the times I was alone many times at Christmas, years ago, yet for some strange reason I was not lonely. At that time my beliefs and convictions were my companions. You will never be lonely for this and so many other reasons.

Love, Dad

Total Life-Support System

December 1, 2005

Mac,

It has been said that our systems are the results of our wiring, including our faith coursing through with tremendous influence. With a visceral, inseparable soul and a genetic predisposition to sooth ourselves, we can better cope with the daily strain of life, and more fully appreciate the great Mystery of it all. Faith affirms life. I recall, when teaching at Amherst, a student asked me if God was a crutch. "Hell no," I replied, "He's a total life-support system!"

Love, Dad

Essence and Love See Beyond Time
December 8, 2005

Mac,

Yesterday was a sad day for a family here in New Hampshire. The father, husband, brother, son, and respected leader in the community suddenly died, only in his mid-forties. He is the brother of Bill Andrews, your ski coach at Cardigan. You noticed I said "is" not "was." The essence of a person is ultimately independent and not contingent upon physical existence, and insofar as it has this freedom, it is superior to existence. That is why we can say that love is stronger than death—that is why we can sing the line from the Christmas carol, "Born that man no more may die" (Wesley, Whitefield & Mendelssohn, 1840) and quote from Scripture, "Nothing can separate us from the love of God, neither things present nor things to come, neither life nor death... in all these things we are more than conquerors."[20] Essence and love see beyond time. The unique being, like all essence, is timeless and imperishable. Pray today that the entire Andrews family will have this assurance now and in the days to come.

Love, Dad

---

20   Romans 8:37-39

North Star
February 25, 2006

Mac,

Last evening the air was cold, crisp and clear. The constellation Ursa Minor could be seen. It is the constellation that contains the North Star. In all areas of life we need a North Star. We need something beyond ourselves to measure our progress, to keep us going in a direction that has our very best as its final port, a bearing that will enable us to look back and assure us that we have traveled well. There will be times, for whatever reason, the clouds or storms will cause us to have difficulty in seeing the North Star but in due time, the clouds vanish and the storms dissipate and there shines the Star, still there, enabling us to go on. For me that North Star has never been a particular church or religious persuasion or a philosophical world view. For me it is the historical person of Jesus of Nazareth, His life and His teaching. His logic is irrefutable, His life is incomparable and His love is irresistible. Travel well with your North Star.

Love, Dad

Mindset
March 6, 2006

Mac,

Mindset: everybody has one, the result of which can be healthy and productive, or unhealthy and destructive—it can be in personal relationships, career, politics, whatever. The student who sees him or herself as not intelligent will live out that mindset; the student who desires to learn, regardless of where they start in the pack, will inevitably do well because their mindset is to learn. I remember a well-known boxing match between Sonny Liston and Muhammad Ali. NOBODY could imagine anything other than Cassius Clay (Ali's name at that time) being annihilated. Liston had it all—size, strength and experience. All Ali seemed to have at that time was a Mouth! He came out at the press conference with the lines:

Float like a butterfly
Sting like a Bee
Your hands can't hit
What your eyes can't see (Clay, 2011)

A famous boxing manager said Ali's fundamentals were all wrong. However, Ali went on to win! Michael Jordan was cut by the high school varsity basketball coach. Later, Jordan's coach at the college level was amazed at the hours he would practice. After the team had lost the last game of the season, Jordan worked for two hours on his jump shot "getting ready for next year." I think it all boils down to Character, Heart and Will. The mindset found in champions on any level is doing your best in learning and improving. You have this *growth mindset*. God bless you.

Love, Dad

Affirmations
March 14, 2006

Mac,

G ood morning! I want to speak today about a life changing principle as fundamental as the law of gravity. More than a century ago a Frenchman by the name of Emile Coue flatly told people that they would feel better and actually be better if they stood in front of a mirror every day and said out loud twice a day, "Every day and in every way, I'm getting better and better." (Coue, 1922) Now a lot of people laughed because they couldn't believe something so simple could have a lasting effect on human life. They were wrong. *Affirmations* [for so they have come to be known] have become a tool for athletes, coaches, psychologists, medical people, those in sales, and basically in all walks of life. The principle is what matters; it is not how others see you, but how you see yourself. If you look closely at the teachings of Jesus, you will discover this principle and see how it impacted the ancient world. To do your own affirmations, stand in front of a mirror (better do this without your roommate around) and say aloud, "I am intelligent, I am in great shape, I make a positive difference upon people, I am a substantive thinker, I do very well when challenged." Whatever you say, do it for thirty days and see what happens. It's not a gimmick; everything of importance which is lasting begins in your mind. Let me know how it changes you in thirty days.

Love, Dad

Results versus Failure

March 16, 2006

Mac,

There is no such thing as failure—there are only results. A great many people in our society have the failure thing running through their mind—a failed relationship, a failed experiment, a failed investment, etc., etc., when, in reality, there are only outcomes and results. People always succeed in getting results. If people try something and they don't get the results they wanted, they've had a learning experience. They take some new actions and produce some new results. It's called the greatest asset, *experience*! People who fear failure make internal representations of what might not work before they even act. This representation is what keeps them from taking the very action that could give them the results they desire. The question to be asked is, "How do you feel about learning?" You can learn from every experience, and thereby always succeed. Mark Twain said, "There is no sadder sight than a young pessimist." (Twain, 1902) He was right. People who succeed don't attach negative emotions to something that doesn't work. They just move on to their next action. I'm glad you are an optimist. The Apostle Paul was a great optimist; he wrote, "We know that all things work together for good."[21] By the way, he wrote that from a prison cell. I'm quite delighted you

---

21 Romans 8:28

have learned this lesson without going to jail. Shakespeare wrote, "Our doubts are traitors, and make us lose the good we oft might win, by fearing to attempt." (Measure for Measure (Act 1, Scene iv), 1604)

Love, Dad

Grass versus Varnish
March 21, 2006

Mac,

Spring is here! Not according to the temperature, but on the calendar! Anyway, it means that soon there will be the smell of grass—it's something that means a lot to me. I never smelled any grass growing up in the city. There was a large varnish company across the street from the house I lived in, so even if there had been a lawn, it would have been overpowered by the smells of the Bissel Varnish Co. Ugh![22] That experience is something that makes me very fond of grass! Perhaps that's one of the reasons I enjoy golf so much. There are many people who focus on things in their past that are like the Bissel Varnish Co. from mine. They can feel it in all their senses. For some reason it becomes their anchor. They never move on and plant grass to fill their senses with new experiences. How are you doing with your supply of lawn seed?

Love, Dad

---

22   When the author was ten years old, he moved with his father and new stepmother into the inner city of Bridgeport, Connecticut, across the street from a varnish company.

Be Watchful After the Victory
May 1, 2006

Mac,

C ongrats on having your squadron marching in at the lead of the Academy parade this weekend.[23] I am reminded of a saintly Presbyterian minister by the name of Andrew Bonar. (To live with a name like that you'd have to be saintly!) Anyway, he said, "Let us be as watchful after the victory as before the battle." (Bonar, n.d.) Often people go through "lows" after great "highs." The reason is they allow their minds to bathe in yesterday rather than the challenge of today. Remember what the Good Book says: "Today is the day the Lord has made; let us rejoice and be glad in it."[24]

Love, Dad

---

23   Under Mac's leadership, his squadron (dorm) was evaluated at the top of the Air Force Academy based on various qualifications. At the full Academy parade just prior to graduation, Mac led his squadron with his ceremonial sabre which he later framed and gave to the author with the inscription: "To My Father, For All The Love and Support, Your Son, Mac."

24   Psalm 118:24

First Salute

The Vigilant, the Active, the Brave
May 3, 2006

Mac,

There are people whose zest for life seems to flag when confronted by unexpected challenges, and there are others who, contrariwise, seem to relish life in the storms which suddenly appear. As unanticipated waves pound these special people, they are lifted high and see precisely what needs to be done and take action accordingly. History bears witness to their virtue. One such individual was Patrick Henry who said, "Sir, we are not weak if we make proper use of those means which the God of Nature has placed in our power . . . The battle, sir, is not to the strong alone, it is to the vigilant, the active, the brave." He went on to say his well-known and often quoted words: "Is life so dear or peace so sweet as to be purchased at the price of chains and slavery? Forbid it, Almighty God. I know not what course others may take, but as for me, give me liberty, or give me death." (Wirt, 1973) It appears that the thoughts and beliefs of such men galvanize the will of the uncommitted and action is undertaken. This kind of leadership is paramount if we are to remain the leaders of the free world. It is this leadership I see in you.

Love, Dad

Mind's Eye
May 18, 2006

Mac,

People are always and properly concerned about taking care of their eyesight. I notice these days that sometimes my arms are not long enough to read the small print without help from glasses! What people don't seem to take equal care about is what they see or don't see with their *mind's eye*. People who, in their mind's eye, can see themselves in good relationships usually experience good relationships. People who see themselves as having a fulfilling vocation or avocation usually do. Imagination of success usually puts into gear the mechanisms of success. Today, check out your mind's eye.

Love, Dad

Integer
October 18, 2006

Mac,

In mathematics, an *integer* is a number that isn't divided into fractions. Just so, a man of integrity isn't divided against himself. He doesn't think one thing and say another, so he's not in conflict with his own principles. You are a walking integer. That is why you talk the walk and walk the talk!

Love, Dad

Assurance
November 19, 2006

Mac,

Assurance is something that everyone desires and so very few have. Assurance of financial security, love, health, belonging, success—the list goes on indefinitely. The reality is that there is little in life that is certain. Shelter can be destroyed in a second by a tornado; finances can be wiped out as in the Great Depression or through foolish investments. How then does one live with uncertainty? The answer— to embrace it! It is the person who is conscious of their mortality that savors every day; it is the person who is aware of the fact that lighting can strike their home that thanks the Good Lord for the warmth of a fireplace and a soft pillow upon retiring for the evening. The great dignity of man is that he/she is not dependent on nor are they the plaything of circumstance, but the conqueror of the vicissitudes of life through choosing to be grateful for this moment, this day. We are deciding beings who this day, as it dawns, can decide among countless possibilities. Being aware of the uncertainty of life helps narrow the choices by placing a value upon how we will use our time.

Love, Dad

Untimely Death
November 26, 2006

Son,

Such horrific news, your squadron mate from the Academy dying the way he did—qualifying to fly F-22s and then to be killed in an automobile accident. Beyond comprehension. His untimely death too, dramatically illustrates that the great tests in life usually come from unexpected sources at unexpected times. I have learned that rising each morning and greeting the day as a gift to be cherished has given me a wealth that is immeasurable. You, your mother and precious friends are my chest of gold. I luxuriate in these treasures, and take none for granted. The sun will set this day and if fortune prevails I will be here to see it rise in the morning. So my son, allow this loss you have experienced to heighten your awareness of the gift of this new day. I await the days ahead with full confidence that your destiny will be realized and make a profound difference in the lives of many. It already has made such a difference in mine.

Love, Dad

Christmas Light
December 1, 2006

Son,

Your mother and I have begun decorating the house and yard in anticipation of Christmas. I appreciate the Christmas story more each year. The event is narrated in Luke's Gospel and that rendition is my favorite, including: "The shepherds were in the field keeping watch over their flocks by night."[25] The word *night* is often overlooked, but I think it suggests something of the darkness of the pre-Christian era. Think of the fact that half the world was in slavery, that women were exploited, that children were exposed when unwanted. Think of the philosophies of the day—the deadly endurance of Stoicism, the indulgence of Epicureanism, and the senselessness of Sophism. Here we can see something of the blackness of the night. Now there is another blackness covering a significant portion of humanity and it is spreading with a zeal that is measurable, and the fountainheads are the radical Islamists who want to rule the world. If the message of Christmas ever needed to be heard, it is now. I know you are a formidable ambassador of that message.

Love, Dad

---

25   Luke 2:8

Gentleness of God in Christmas
December 14, 2006

Mac,

One of the aspects I love about Christmas is that there is a gentleness about God that is revealed in the Nativity. He who holds the sun in the hollow of His hand, who takes up isles as a very little thing, who counts the nations as but dust in the balance, is also the Gentle One. Much like the wide, deep ocean, that pulsates into every bay and blesses the pastures with dew and rain, so God's heart throbs and pulsates to the uttermost parts of the universe, having a parent's feeling for His children. Great is the genius of Plato, Bacon, and Pascal or James, revealing itself in tides of thought, but greater and richer is the genius of the heart that is conscious of the vast fountains of love poured forth in generous tides before the God whose throne is mercy, whose strength is gentleness, whose considerateness is our pledge of pardon, peace and life eternal. These are just some of the reasons Christmas means so much to me.

Love, Dad

Plugged In

January 15, 2007

Son,

Augustine said prayer is awareness of God's Presence. The Lord assures us, "Ask and you shall receive; seek and you shall find; knock and it will be opened to you.[26] Whatever you ask in my name will be done."[27] I think it's sort of like an electrical outlet. Behind every outlet is this mysterious thing called electrical power. Light a home, heat a room, show a movie and so on. The outlet of course doesn't do anything unless we're "plugged in." We are assured that the power of God is there to lighten, to free, to guide, to strengthen, to mend and to love. To pray is another way of getting plugged into the outlet.

Love, Dad

---

26   Matthew 7:7
27   John 14:13

No Mask

February 3, 2007

Son,

What psychology has done is to bring scientific terminology to the truths the Bible presents in poetry, allegory and parable. "Where your treasure is, there will your heart be also."[28] Of course! What we shall love is the key problem of human existence, because we tend to become the reflection of what we love. Does a person love money? Then their values will be materialistic. Does a person love power? Then the aggressive instincts in them will slowly become more dominant. Does a person love God and their neighbor? Then they're not likely to need a psychiatrist! Perhaps my favorite passage that reflects the wisdom of the Bible is in John: "And you shall know the truth and the truth shall set you free."[29] Nine out of ten people who came to see me over the years were tormented by guilt, exhausted by unresolved hate and countless other anxieties because they didn't know the truth about themselves. The job of a psychologist is to remove the camouflage of self-deception. Only the brave can take off the camouflage. That is why many prefer masking themselves all their lives. I'm proud of the fact you don't wear a mask.

Love, Dad

---

28 Matthew 6:21
29 John 8:32

Discouragement versus Gratitude
February 7, 2007

Son,

Well, what a surprise! I end up in the hospital with internal bleeding.[30] Most people would be surprised and perhaps discouraged. The good news is nothing catches our Lord by surprise and that we live in an age of great medical accomplishments. It's all in how you look at things. The way I look at this is with gratitude that I live in a day and age when things like this can be attended to with dispatch! Oftentimes I tell people I see that discouragement and gratitude are mutually exclusive. The easiest thing to overcome is discouragement by being grateful. I am grateful you are my son.

Love, Dad

---

30 The author slipped on snow-covered ice while on his cell phone with Mac, walking the new puppy Gus (nicknamed for Caesar Augustus). After the fall, he developed severe internal bleeding.

Gates of Splendor
February 9, 2007

Son,

G etting blood transfusions today, for whatever reason, made me think of a book I read many years ago called *Through Gates of Splendor.*[31] It was the true story of Jim Elliott who was with MAF, (Missionary Aviation Fellowship). He flew into the Amazon to witness to the natives who lived there. He was attacked and killed. His diary was recovered and in it were these words: "A man is no fool to give up what he cannot keep to gain what he cannot lose." (Elliot, 1978) Truer words were never spoken. To engage in significant friendships, significant work, significant charities—these are the things that can never be taken away or lost. So Elliott's words are profoundly sensible. I love the fact that you have followed in the same sensible path.

Love, Dad (Dictated to Mom)

---

31   The hospital had been unable to stop the author's internal bleeding and, in addition to dictating this thought for the day, the author also planned his memorial "coronation" service, *just in case.*

Staying Centered

February 20, 2007

Son,

There was a song written a long time ago that had as its theme the lyrics, "The fundamental things of life apply, *as time goes by.*" (Hupfeld, 1931) With this hospitalization, I have been reminded of this truth. One may be prone—in light of the change that is constantly confronting us in areas of science, medicine, global politics, etc., to forget the theme of this song. Yet, the value of relationships, love, intimacy, character, the wonder of creation, all these "remain the same." The key to conscious awareness of this truth is *staying centered.* While in itself rather basic, staying centered involves a commitment of time. The challenge is rather formidable. So many noisy demands compete for our attention: the ring of the telephone, social obligations, work, general business, all things which need attending and—while are perhaps good and necessary—can crowd or displace this time commitment which allows us to be our best. Why is it that, as some grow older, they lose the playful exuberance of childhood or the fascination with the mysterious nature of things and the natural inquisitiveness of youth? I do believe that as one stays centered, these qualities can be part of our daily experience regardless of how much "time goes by." Your rituals, starting each day with these thoughts for today, are designed to maintain this youthful enthusiasm. With this perspective, the best is yet to come! I believe this to be the case for you and for me.

Love, Dad

But if not . . .

February 21, 2007

Son,

G reat to be home, great to be able to talk with you. Many people prayed for my physical wellbeing, and they continue to do so, for which I am indeed grateful. While in the hospital I had many thoughts about many things, one of which was "What if I don't make it?" Without going into detail, suffice it to say that I was at peace with either outcome. I recalled a passage of Scripture from the Old Testament story of Daniel where three of his fellow Hebrew exiles were threatened to be put into the fiery furnace if they would not worship King Nebuchadnezzar's idol, thereby renouncing their faith. Their reply showed a great deal about them and their faith. In the face of the threat, they said, "Our God is able to deliver us out of the furnace... *But if not*, we will not serve your gods or worship your golden image."[32] I never forgot that story. I always want to be a "But if not" kind of guy. I just figure He knows best. However, I sure am glad He got me through this particular furnace! Have a wonderful day!

Love, Dad

---

32   Daniel 3:17-18

Bumps in the Path

February 22, 2007

Son,

Good to be back in the library in the early a.m., although not as early as usual . . .
I remember, as a little boy, going for a visit to some relative in Canada. At the time I was living in Buffalo having been returned after the kidnapping. The relative lived on a farm which had some woods at the end of the clearing. Someone else and I decided to go exploring. There appeared to be a path up the side of a steep hill and I said, "Let's climb up." My cousin (or whoever it was) said, "That's no path; it's all rocky and bumpy!" My reply was, "The bumps are what you climb on." These past few weeks have been for me the bumps to climb on. A great many people don't know what to do when they encounter bumps on the pathway of life, but according to the Good Book these can be stepping stones to a much more fulfilling life, a clearer perspective and a greater awareness of the Grace of God. I trust whatever bumps you may come across will lead you to greater heights than you have ever known.

Love, Dad

Size of the Candle

February 24, 2007

Son,

L ast evening I received a phone call from someone who had just returned from Paris where they had gone to the Cathedral of Notre Dame. While there, they had their two grandchildren light two candles and say a prayer for me (re: my surgery). She said on the phone she was anxious to know how it went. When I told her it was successful, she said she was relieved! This was due to the fact she was feeling guilty about buying the cheapest candles! I loved it! Someday we'll have a talk about *intention* and how that, in a miraculous way, is what prayer is all about. God doesn't care about the size of the candle! It's all about *intention*. Isn't that a great thought?!

Love, Dad 20/20 [33]

---

33   The author's reference to his goal of living to at least until 2020.

PILOT TRAINING
INTO THE WILD BLUE YONDER

When Mac graduated from Pilot Training, he asked his father to pin on his wings as part of the official ceremony.

Dollar Ride
August 27, 2007

Son,

One of the things the astronauts did in 1968 (Frank Borman, Jim Lovell and Bill Anders) as they circled the moon was to read from Genesis and other parts of the Bible, to *sacramentalize* that experience—to transmit somehow what they were experiencing to everyone back on earth. I've learned that we do not need to circle the moon to *sacramentalize* the events in our life: a morning sunrise, evening sunset, a look into our loved ones eyes, a special touch when heart and soul becomes one with another—all can be sacred and indeed are. As you lift off and feel the surge of your plane and feel as if you can "reach out and touch the face of God," (Magee, circa 1941) sense the sacrament in which you are partaking.[34]

Love, Dad

---

34 "Dollar Ride" and "Fini Flight" (see page 279) refer to the longstanding Air Force tradition of naming and celebrating a pilot's first and last flights in various aircraft.

Mindfulness

January 1, 2008

Son,

Today is the first day of opportunity for a new year—not just new in the sense of another, like one that passed by, but new in a qualitative sense, different than that which went before. In this sense we look forward with an optimism that is grounded in a new reality. It's much different than wishful thinking for it is all about the in-depth substance of mindfulness. You see, mindfulness has to do with the ever-expanding capacity to be fully present in whatever we are doing or thinking. We can be engaged in conversation, piloting a magnificent aircraft, or sipping a cup of tea. Therefore, as we evolve with the emergence of a new year it is not just a repeat of another year, it is the depth we can bring, a depth which was previously impossible, for indeed we are different. So while experiences will perhaps be novel, that is not what will be the difference. The difference will be us, you and me. It is so because we are alive, we are growing, changing, deepening our appreciation of this magnificent creation, of life, of love, of each breath we take. A concentration of mindfulness. So with all of this and much more, I wish you a magnificent new year.

Love, Dad

Positive Self-Talk

January 4, 2008

Son,

The classic from Norman Vincent Peale emphasized *The Power of Positive Thinking.* Many people at the time thought his suggestion was like whistling while walking past a cemetery! It won't change anything but your feelings! Yet, according the Mayo Clinic, positive thinkers (optimistic individuals) enjoy a host of health benefits including:

1. Longer life span
2. Lower rates of depression
3. Greater resistance to colds
4. Better coping skills in the face of challenges
5. Better physiological and psychological well-being.

The clinic also deduced that negative thoughts or positive thoughts go hand in hand with negative or positive self-talk. All of this of course is a *no brainer.* It appears that Peale is becoming more appealing than appalling to the so-called shrink industry! The good news is that you learned a long time ago that you can, *if you think you can.* The best is yet to come!

Love, Dad

Spiritual World View
January 13, 2008

Son,

Yesterday I had an interesting conversation. The individual with whom I was speaking was about to leave for a visit with his only sibling, a sister with pancreatic cancer. He said this would be the last time he would see her. This individual has a science background, worked for the CIA, computer whiz, etc., etc. When he said, "This will be the last time I will ever see her," my response was that his perception of the "last time" was based upon an incorrect World View. At that moment he was caught. He looked at me with that expression which said, "What the hell are you talking about?" I said, "If you are a physicalist, believing that a person is just a collection of atoms, cells, neurons, etc., I could see how you would feel this is the last time. However, if you believe that a person is fundamentally a spiritual being in a physical body, then the body dying is not the end of the person." I then went on to tell him that indeed that is what he believed but that it was not consciously the way he was seeing things at the moment. I reminded him that the things we admire most about people is their compassion, humor, forgiveness, empathy, love—all the attributes that have nothing to do with cells and tissue and ligaments! We even say of these people that they are wonderfully *humane*, (translation: what makes them human.) So that which makes us unique has nothing to do with our bodies.

"And God breathed into man the breath of life, and man became a living soul."[35] Have a great day.

Love, Dad

---

35   Genesis 2:7

Patton on Prayer
February 10, 2008

Son,

I loved the pictures you sent of your last flight. I can sense your passion for your calling to serve. One of the most passionate military men in our country's history was, as you know, General George S. Patton. When he died, the *New York Times* wrote, "He was deeply religious and incredibly profane," (McLaughlin, 1945, p. 18) and President Eisenhower said the mention of Patton's name struck fear into his enemies. His soldiers who fought under his command loved him and reporters said they would see tears flowing liberally when he spoke to how much he was counting on them. Many stories have been written both positively and negatively about him. He was seen as calloused and tender, arrogant and humble, but no one wanted to fight against him! In one of the scenes of the movie about his life, a German Commander said that a man who both prays and swears curses really worried him! I want to end with this quote from Patton himself as he addressed his men, "I urge all of you men to pray, not alone in church, but everywhere. Pray when driving. Pray when fighting. Pray alone. Pray with others. Pray by night and pray by day. Pray for the defeat of our wicked enemy whose god is aggression. Pray for victory. Pray for peace. We must march together, all out for God." (Patton, 1944)

Love, Dad

You Bring the Uniqueness
April 2, 2008

Son,

It's getting closer and closer until you take off in a C-17. Very, very exciting! The key that I see in you and others in various professions is the following: it does not lie in the particular profession; it lies within us. The manner in which we do the job is what matters, and it has always been this way. We bring the uniqueness of our existence, as the Germans say, to the *Sitz im leben* or, 'life situation.' The "who we are" is that which validates the life situation regardless of the profession. The indispensability and irreplaceability, the singularity and uniqueness issue from the person, from you. There are other pilots, other medical doctors, other financial experts, but there is only one you. That is and will remain the most unique and significant aspect of your work. You have not withheld any part of yourself, intellectually, emotionally or physically. Because of this, you are reaping rewards that many will never know. You have won the respect, admiration and confidence of your peers. You have committed yourself to *Whatever it Takes.*

Love, Dad (W.I.T. – Whatever It Takes)

Listen to the Whispers
April 20, 2008

Son,

Being out west for a few days, I came across a Cherokee proverb: "Listen to the whispers and you won't have to listen to the screams." I really like this because it applies to all areas of life, whether it's taking care of your body, equipment, mind or people! Today, have some quiet time, enough so as to hear the whispers.

Love, Dad

Defining Moments
April 21, 2008

Son,

Defining moments are those moments that determine the kind of person we are becoming and will become. They can be good or bad, painful or gratifying, or they can even give us an opportunity to turn, change direction and seek a new destination. I can point to many defining moments in my own life. The thing about defining moments is that they can happen at any time and serve as an intersection in our lives. These defining moments can be personal or professional, but always involve a choice—onward and upward or backward and downward. They aren't always dramatic or public. They can be as simple as staying home and preparing for tomorrow, or goofing off and facing the new challenge without putting in the time. It would appear to me that the choices you have made in your own defining moments have won the respect and admiration of those who observe you but, more importantly, have won the respect of the man in the mirror.

Love, Dad

Expectations
April 23, 2008

Son,

I have discovered that our lives are shaped not as much by our experiences as by our expectations. Expectations are a way of using imagination, hard work and perseverance. This is the best way of overcoming odds. Someday I will tell you about a teacher I had by the name of Phyllis Gaffney. She told me in the 9th grade I should only take "shop" courses. "Couldn't handle academics," was her thesis regarding me. As you know, after your mother and I were married for just three weeks, she was shot, and the doctor said she wouldn't survive. In retrospect, I guess I really never did believe in so-called "odds."

Love, Dad

Pakistani Prayer
April 29, 2008

Son,

I recall a time when I was in Pakistan. I was going out into a village some thirty to forty miles outside of Islamabad. The driver of the vehicle (a small bus) stood in front of the van and clasped his hands as if in prayer and bowed his head. I thought to myself, "He must be praying thankfully for his mode of transportation." After about half an hour, he stopped. He pulled off to the side of the road. There he lifted up the hood and said some things I didn't understand. He then walked down to the stream. Coming back with a pail of water, he poured it into the radiator, which had gone dry. A while later, he again stopped the vehicle. The driver stood in the road, waved to another passing van, which stopped. After discussion, the driver of the other vehicle got a container off the back of his vehicle and brought it over to ours. It was gasoline. My conclusion: if you are going to pray with thanksgiving for your vehicle, make sure you have water in the radiator and gasoline in your tank!

Love, Dad

Confidence Intentionality
May 20, 2008

Son,

I loved hearing how well your sim[36] went yesterday. Seeing how you have chosen to relax on the golf course in between your flights (a great choice by the way), I have a quote for you from Bobby Jones: "Without confidence, a golfer is little more than a hacker." (Rotella, Bob & Cullen, Bob, 2004) A confident golfer thinks about what he wants to happen on the course. A golfer who lacks confidence thinks about the things he doesn't want to happen. That's all confidence is. While this was written about golf, it applies to just about any profession. Rollo May, a psychologist well respected by me and many others, speaks with great depth about the importance of intentionality. He basically draws the conclusion that a healthy person is able to have clear intentions and chooses to act upon them. They (the healthy) say, in essence, "Yes, I will even have it so!" It's the attitude of the jock who says, "Bring it on!" You have demonstrated this attitude since the first time you stepped on to the Academy terrazzo. I know it will continue to serve you well.

Love, Dad

---

36   Simulator – a suspended enclosed structure with highly accurate mock cockpit which can simulate various flight conditions and emergency situations, used as a training tool.

Learn to Surf

June 9, 2008

Son,

There is a Zen teacher by the name of Oesel Tendzin who said, "You can't stop the waves, but you can learn to surf. One person will struggle with the waves and be battered about. Another person will learn to ride with them. Same waves, different experiences." (Parent, 2002) I see some golfers experience a meltdown if they have a bad hole. I simply think, "How should I ride this wave?" I'm delighted you have learned to surf!

Love, Dad

What Lies Within
June 10, 2008

Son,

The great religions, philosophies and psychologies of the world all point to the fact that we need to, at one time, look within. Many, if not most, are hesitant to take this step because they have been wounded and do not believe they have the strength or the resources to move on, to change, to transcend, to achieve. In addition many feel their wounds are deserved and thus "accept" emptiness as their "just deserts." How depressing! It's depressing because all the resources to know fulfillment are present and available. Jesus said, "The Kingdom of God is within you."[37] An infinite number of spiritual laws exist and they govern the structures, forces and patterns of all existence— and all point to a realm of higher reality. All these laws have the power to change our lives. Some believe these laws come from the Great Spirit, some believe they come from the Creator or are simply the mechanics of the universe. For me the teachings of Jesus are irrefutable and His message of love irresistible. It was Thoreau or Emerson who said, "What lies before us and what lies behind us are small matters compared to what lies within us. And when we bring what is within out into the world, miracles happen."[38]

Love, Dad

---

37 Luke 17:21
38 This quote has been commonly but erroneously attributed to Thoreau and Emerson by many varied persons but was most likely penned by Henry S. Haskins in "Meditations on Wall Street," published in 1940.

Co-Creation of our Destiny
June 13, 2008

Son,

I think my having this medical challenge (rotator cuff surgery) is wonderful in one sense. More than ever I realize that we are biological creations of Divine design. Once this realization becomes part of our conscious mind, we can never again live an ordinary life. Who wants to be ordinary anyway? If this be the case, then every thought that crosses our mind, every belief we nurture, every memory to which we cling translates into a positive or negative command and produces an energy infusion—positive or negative—to our body and spirit. Magnificent to contemplate, but yikes, scary as hell as well! In a sense we are co-creators of our destiny! Co-creation is in essence a characteristic of spiritual adulthood. I am awfully thankful that Grace enters into the equation for the occasional dumb decisions I make. The path to empowerment is basic; one must be committed to turning dung into fertilizer. Nothing magical, just a growth choice—a secret you learned early on.

Love, Dad

Sacred Partnership
June 21, 2008

Son,

There is a wonderful implication to the word *partnership*. In today's society it is thought of in terms of business ventures, marriage, organizational structures, etc. However when you use the concept in terms of *Weltanschauung*, or one's worldview, the implication is even more dramatic. For instance, in the Christian faith one believes in a Creator. All that is, is a result of the creative energy of the God of the universe. This is why Einstein believed that there was an intelligence behind the forces of existence. He said in a vivid manner, "I, at any rate, am convinced that He [God] is not playing at dice." (Born, 2005) What the Scriptures teach is that there is another part of creation, not just in the physical sense but in terms of our life at its core. We are co-creators with this God of the Universe. We co-create by the choices we make. Awesome! Now this kind of partnership is incredibly reassuring, for when we feel inadequate or need guidance or need to know someone has our back or is a wingman that is covering our *flight of life*, He's there. Now this is the kind of partnership that gives us an unbelievable sense of peace.

Love, Dad

Love, Learn, Laugh, Labor
June 24, 2008

Son,

Another day with new opportunities to learn, to laugh, to love and to labor. It seems like yesterday that I sat in front of our stone fireplace in Bridgewater and shared with you these simple truths. If I recall, you were about ten years old. I had given a talk at Pike Industries, and these were the four points I had made to their executive team. The thrust of my lecture was that fulfillment depended upon these principles. These truths seemed so real and important to me that I repeatedly stressed them over and over to you as part of our evening ritual. You have embraced them in your core, and I am fully confident that whatever the future days may bring, these will serve as pillars in your daily life. Since that time I have shared these thoughts with others, and they have been well received. But I am not sure they have become a way of life for others as they have for you. So my son, whatever you may have heard or will hear in future days, from me or anyone else, the riches that will come your way from daily experiencing these four simple principles will keep your inner man in great health and richness.

Love, Dad

Choose Wisely
July 11, 2008

Son,

You know how I feel about the power of choice. Managing the power of choice, with all its creative and spiritual implications, is the essence of the human experience. All teachers, gurus, mentors and shrinks worth anything, all direct us to recognize that the power to make choices is the dynamic that converts our spirits into matter, for choice is the process of creation itself. When [our dog] Pooh Bear had to be put down and you and I took him to the veterinarian, you taught me a lot about choices. As we were sitting in the truck afterward, I was crying, and you were smiling. I asked, "What's going on?" Your reply was, "I'm thinking of all the times Pooh Bear made me laugh." That was your way of choosing on how to deal with the loss of our beautiful dog! You had to be all of eight years old! Ever since then you have seen how choices empower a person to deal with disappointment, delight, victories or whatever. As the old Knight said in *Indiana Jones and the Last Crusade*, "You have chosen wisely." (Spielberg, 1989) Choose to have a great day.

Love, Dad, W.I.T.

Tony Snow

July 14, 2008

Son,

A few days ago a rather remarkable man, Tony Snow, came to the end of what I refer to as his "earth time." He was fifty-three years old and had served as a TV talk-show host, radio commentator, journalist, writer and press secretary for the president of the United States. He will be remembered not for the many jobs he had but for the person he was while conducting these assignments. Intelligence, grace, humor, candor and openness were his characteristics. He leaves behind a wife and three young children. Listening to people talk about him brought home forcefully that who we are is uniquely more important than what we do. A year ago he gave the commencement address at a college and said some of the following: "Today is an important day, not only in terms of a diploma, but the beginning of escalating accomplishments. Here are some tips. First, think. Secondly, don't play it safe, but rise to the occasion. Third, summon faith in God, your friends and in yourself. Faith is as natural as the air we breathe; it is the ultimate extreme sport. Wherever you are, and whatever you do, you've got the breath of life. A precious blessing . . . and while God doesn't promise tomorrow he does promise Eternity." (Snow, 2007) So now, my son, he has heard the joyous words of our Savior, "Well done good and faithful servant, enter now into the joy of your Master."[39] Choose to have a great day.

Love, Dad

---

39   Matthew 25:21

Congratulations C-17 Pilot
July 15, 2008

Son,

C ongratulations are in order, for you are now a C-17 pilot. I know that for these past many months you've been training for this day. The journey covered a lot of ground, beginning with a dream sustained by enthusiasm, fueled by hard work and preparation, and accomplished by a tenacity of spirit! You have chosen to serve our country in this time of war with discipline and honor. John McCain wrote in his book *Faith of My Fathers*, "Nothing is more liberating than to fight for a cause larger than yourself, something that encompasses you but is not defined by your existence alone." (McCain & Salter, 1999) At a young age you have discovered that meaning in life is formed by thoughts and actions around a purpose that makes your life of most worth. As Nietzsche said, "He who has a 'why' to live for can bear almost any how." (Nietzsche, 1911) Well done. As you turn another page in your career, you do so with our pride and gratitude for the warrior you are.

Love, Dad

LABOR

2008 - 2011

INTO HARM'S WAY

No Traffic Jams
July 17, 2008

Son,

R oger Staubach was one was one of the most admired NFL players of all time. He was a graduate of the Naval Academy and went on to play quarterback for the Dallas Cowboys when they were "America's Team." At an after-dinner speech, he made the following statement: "There are no traffic jams along the extra mile." (Hyken, 2016) A pretty astute observation!

Love, Dad

Success According to Schweitzer
July 23, 2008

Son,

H ere is something Albert Schweitzer [commonly attributed] said that reminds me of you:

"Success is not the key to happiness. Happiness is the key to success. If you love what you are doing, you will be successful." (Schweitzer, 1947) Schweitzer also stated, "The only ones among you who will really be happy are those who have sought and found how to serve."

Love, Dad

Laughter
August 9, 2008

Son,

I have always believed that laughter is perhaps the most powerful healing agent in existence. Happy thoughts make happy molecules! I have seen that for some unknown reason (to me) my hair chooses to grow in my ears, on my shoulders, chest and in my nose rather than on my head! My attitude: so be it! Our bodies are like a garage in which we park our soul, or as I like to say, our core. The garage serves a purpose, but what it houses is far more valuable than the garage itself. Keep the garage in good shape, but value your core. Choose to have a good day.

Love, Dad

Willie Mays
August 11, 2008

Son,

Willie Mays, who I saw play for the New York Giants and who is in the Hall of Fame, said the following: "It isn't hard to be good from time to time in sports. What is tough is being good every day." [commonly attributed] Rituals and choices are key in being in the only Hall of Fame that counts for Eternity.

Love, Dad

Universal Spirit
August 12, 2008

Son,

Robert Burns penned the following lines: "O that God would give us the grace to see ourselves as others see us." (Burns, 1787) Sounds good at first glance, yet I have discovered that many people lose their authenticity because they are too concerned with how others perceive them! Worry about the opinion of others can lead to conformity to the social mores or the culture of the day, which are constantly evolving. The interesting teaching of all great religions is that there is a universal spirit within everyone. The problem is that people get out of touch with that Spirit and lose the genius that makes them unique. Born an original, they die a carbon copy. The key to maintaining our unique self is taking time to being in contact with the Creator who is within us. Walt Whitman, the great poet, said it this way: "[It is] perhaps the deepest, most eternal thought latent in the human soul. This is the thought of God, merged in the thoughts of moral right and the immortality of the soul. Great, great is this thought—aye, greater than all else." (Whitman, 1892) Once a person embraces this truth, there are no limits, for the Source that causes the universe to exist, that same Source is within us.

Love, Dad

No Barriers

August 21, 2008

Son,

While in Florida I went to an aquarium where a savage barracuda and a Spanish mackerel were placed in the same glass tank with a glass partition separating them. Unaware of this barrier, the barracuda quickly tried to attack the mackerel but was stopped by the partition. After repeatedly bumping his nose, the barracuda finally quit trying. Later the partition was removed, but the barracuda would swim only to the point where the barrier had been and stopped, because he thought it was still there! Many people are like the barracuda—they move forward until they reach an imaginary barrier, but then stop because of a self-imposed limitation based on past experience. The only limit on any man's growth and progress is the limit he places on himself by his own thinking.

Love, Dad

Just Do It
August 22, 2008

Son,

The Nike ad that I like the best is the one which simply says, "Just Do It." No frills, no sweet talk, it's straightforward. This is the attitude it takes to be the best. Abraham Maslow, who I feel is one of the best ever (for he didn't gain insight by studying whack jobs but people who were the best at what they did), said the following, and I'm paraphrasing here: "To want to be the best you are capable of becoming—that is the only path that is worth taking. If you don't do this then I warn you, you will be deeply unhappy for the rest of your life. You will be evading your own capacities." I would dare to say the people who came up with the Nike ad would agree! Not "Do I feel like giving it my all today?" or "I'd rather be in bed" or anything else—*just do it*. This is what it takes to be your best and you have it! Go for it today.

Love, Dad

Destiny
September 26, 2008

Son,

William Jennings Bryan said it this way: "Destiny is not a matter of chance; it is a matter of choice; it is not a thing to be waited for, it is a thing to be achieved." (Bryan, 1899) Sound remotely familiar?

Love, Dad

Extra Baggage
November 17, 2008

Son,

It will be great to see you later this week. With the airlines charging money for baggage these days, it's interesting to hear people discuss what they really need, over against what may be considered extra baggage. I have found in life there are a great many people who live daily with extra baggage: resentment for that which they won't let go, a victim mentality, jealousy, preoccupation with things, blame avoidance, living in the past, and the list goes on. It would really do people good if they realized that everything they actually need is more than likely present all the time. There really is an extra price to pay when lugging all the other *stuff.* The Scriptures tell us, "My God shall supply all your needs according to His abundant riches in Christ Jesus our Lord."[40] When a person sees every day as an opportunity to love, learn, laugh and labor, luggage is not an issue.

Love, Dad

---

40   Philippians 4:19

Connected and Centered

December 27, 2008

Son,

It was a great gift you brought to me this Christmas—namely, yourself. Being with you was indeed a blessing, it was fun and it was sobering. You are purposeful and prepared for what lies ahead. I have great confidence that you will not be caught off guard. Staying *connected* and *centered* are the two keys you have embraced, and they will serve you exceedingly well. In the letter you gave to me on Christmas morning[41], you referred to your deployment as a "sacred duty." There is in the Holy Scriptures a reference to the perspective you possess, for it says, "Whatsoever

---

41   After his Christmas at home, Mac left for a five-month deployment. Here is what his handwritten letter, dated on Christmas Day of that year, said: "Father, It is with great confidence and a sense of purpose that I write you this note. In a few days I will be traveling across the oceans and engaging once again in that 'great and noble tradition' of which you spoke of so many years ago. And while the physical distance between us will be great, I know that in spirit we are inseparable. I have benefitted much over the past decade from your daily words of inspiration. Among those many lessons you have taught me the importance of remaining centered and having that inner peace which is so necessary when facing the trials and tribulations of life. Keeping this in mind I know that I will overcome any obstacle that is placed in my path. I go forth to fulfill my sacred duty armed with this knowledge and the support of unconditional love. As Always, Your Son, Mac"

you do in word and deed, do all to the Glory of God."[42] You have made this perspective part of who you are, and my heart overflows with joy when I reflect on your sense of commitment. Every morning during your deployment, I will reread your letter and bring you in my prayers before the throne of Grace. Also in the Scriptures there is a promise given to another young warrior by the name of Joshua. He was about to undertake a mission of critical importance, as are you. This was the promise: "As I have been with Moses, so I will be with you . . . be strong and of good courage for the LORD your God is with you wherever you go."[43] So, my son, go with a peaceful heart and the fortifying assurance that you do not go alone.

With a heart filled with love, Dad

---

42   1 Corinthians 10:31
43   Joshua 1:5, 9

Band of Brothers
December 28, 2008

Son,

The History Channel yesterday played the series *The Band of Brothers*. I had seen most of the series when it was originally shown on HBO. Obviously a different time in history, a different war, a different world. But your 16th Squadron has become in a sense your own band of brothers. Tomorrow morning at 0700 you will gather together and be air lifted to your deployment. Five months from now you will come back. At your core you will be the same; however, your perspective will be different. You will be a seasoned veteran. You will have much to offer, your insights will deepen and your appreciation of Grace will be richer and fuller. You have had a history of leadership throughout your academic and military experience—from Cardigan Mountain School, to the Brooks School, to the Air Force Academy, and through Flight School at Vance and Altus. I am confident that this attribute will continue to manifest itself and evolve to an even higher level. The simple things of life will take on an attractiveness that will be impossible to overlook. You will enrich the lives of those with whom you come into contact in a most significant manner, for this is your gift. So leave tomorrow as the warrior with a peaceful heart. This is the beginning of another wonderful chapter in your life. Without a doubt it will be a bestseller.

With love and confidence in you and your band of brothers,

Dad

Mac's Band of Brothers

Flying over a mountain range of Afghanistan

Awareness

December 29, 2008

Son,

The key in the months that lie ahead will be *awareness*: awareness of your equipment, awareness of your flight mates, awareness of the circumstances (weather, bad guys, etc.), and awareness of your Heavenly Father, Who is committed to your well-being, and Who is your Co-Pilot in all of life's circumstances. Many people go through life without this awareness and thus do not reach their God-given potential. This awareness is the key to peace of heart and clear thinking. Cogency of thought and consistency of performance will be the result. So my son, as you leave the States this morning and fly to your duty station, rest assured that our prayer will be that this awareness will be a constant in your life.

Love, Dad

Qatar Hypernikon
December 30, 2008

Son,

B y now you are in Qatar! About the size of Connecticut in area, but definitely not anywhere near good old New England. I trust that the trip was uneventful. I just reread your Christmas note to me, which you appropriately placed in the box of cigars under the Christmas tree! The line that jumped out at me was the one in which you wrote, "And while the physical distance between us will be great I know that in spirit we are inseparable." It will be this reality that I will focus upon. You may or may not know that this was one of the great truths taught by the greatest teacher ever, namely, Jesus. He set it in stone, or should I say in His blood, when after the crucifixion He told His disciples to "go into the uttermost parts of the world"[44] and said that He would be with them always.[45] He was laying forth the foundation block of a spiritual reality: in essence, when you touch another person with love, you are joined forever! Later on, one of His followers put it this way: "So faith, hope and love abide, these three; but the greatest of these is love"[46] and "nothing can separate us from the love of God . . . neither things present nor things to come,

---

44   Acts 1:8b
45   Matthew 28:20b
46   1 Corinthians 13:13

for in all these things we are more than conquerors!"[47] It is one of the great Greek words you learned so long ago: *hypernikon* or "more than conqueror"! That is precisely what we have in you.

Love, Dad

---

47   Romans 8:37-39

Humor
January 3, 2009

Son,

I hope that, with all that is going on in your missions and deployment, you find something to smile about every day. I recall when President Reagan was shot in an attempted assassination; he was rushed to the hospital and wheeled into the emergency room at George Washington University Hospital. He looked up at the doctors and said, "I hope you're all Republicans"! (At the time he was seventy years old!) When he awoke, a nurse was holding his hand and the first thing he said to her was, "Does Nancy know about us?" His humor had a way of putting everyone at ease in this critical situation. Sometimes the best way to make sure people do their best in an otherwise tense situation is to make them feel relaxed. I am confident that with your natural sense of humor you will be able to put your crewmates at ease so that they can do their best. Being who you are has been, and will continue to be, the greatest asset you bring to any situation.

Love, Dad

A Father's Prayer

January 4, 2009

Son,

T his TFT is a little different because it is not a thought as I normally write; it is my prayer to God for you:

Dear God, You have promised that if we come to You in prayer, You will respond to us and hear our prayer. My prayer today, Heavenly Father, is on behalf of my son. I am confident in Your love for him and I know that Your love is a perfect love. I pray not just for him in his essence, because I know that he is inseparable from You in that regard; I pray for him in terms of his humanity, his physical well-being, his mental well-being, his decisiveness, his clarity of mind, his physical strength, his indomitable spirit, his eyes, his arms and legs, his broad shoulders, every aspect of his physicality. I pray that he indeed will have a peace that passes all understanding, that his confidence in that which he has learned, and disciplined himself to diligently pursue, will give him a quietness in the midst of the storms of war. I pray that he will have an overwhelming sense of You, dear Heavenly Father. And I pray for him and his fellow pilots that You will keep them from harm in these terrible and demanding days. I pray these things in the name of Jesus our Lord. Amen.

Son, I wanted you to know how I am praying for you.

Love, Dad

Friends

January 9, 2009

Son,

A man's growth is seen in the expanding choir of his friends. You have made a habit of choosing friends well. The result is that you have helped one another simply by being together— listening, challenging, competing, laughing, sharing—in spite of most of them working in an incredibly demanding profession. Step by step we all scale a mysterious ladder; doing it alone is always dangerous. I learned as a volunteer firefighter that having someone to "foot" the ladder is always the best way to go as we seek to reach new heights. You have had choice companions, and all of you at times have footed the ladder for each other. Without choice friends, an ocean of opportunity turns into a shallow, muddy pond. You have accomplished much because you have chosen wisely in the critical area of quality relationships.

Love, Dad

Best Friends

Courage
January 15, 2009

Son,

As I reread your account of landing through a small hole of heavy cloud cover in mountainous terrain, only to have the landing area appear, disappear and then at the last possible moment reappear (amazing!) all I could think and feel is admiration for the daily bravery and courage you and others are constantly demonstrating. I do believe that this kind of courage is conceived in the daily choices that are made long before the event. I am reminded of something Emerson wrote: "Valor consists in the power of self-recovery, so that a man cannot have his flank turned, cannot be out-generalled, but put him where you will, he stands. There are degrees of idealism. We first learn it academically, as the magnet was once a toy. Then we see it in youth. Then its countenance waxes stern and grand, and we see that it must be true." (Emerson, [Circles], 1909) It is manhood at its best. No surprise and I would expect nothing less from you.

Love, Dad, W.I.T. (Whatever It Takes)

Hudson River Landing
January 16, 2009

Son,

Yesterday a plane landed in the Hudson River. It had sucked in Canada geese upon take off. Both engines! Everybody since then has been talking about the "miracle" that nobody was killed or seriously hurt. Let me tell you some details. The pilot who was flying the plane decided (when both engines were in flames) he had to put down, and the only place where there were no buildings was the river. The miracle did have a special instrument: the pilot. He had been an F-4 pilot in the Air Force and had been flying for US Air since the 1980s. It's amazing how many miracles take place when the people involved are well trained, experienced, intelligent and professional. When I think of these qualities, it causes me to be so grateful that you are this kind of instrument. I am confident that the troops you supply and transport to and from special places thank the Good Lord for your part in their own personal deliverance. Not from a river but a gigantic and dangerous sandbox. Proud of you.

Love, Dad, W.I.T.

Emotions
March 19, 2009

Son,

I believe in emotions, a whole range of emotions: everything from joy, satisfaction, awe, pride, anger, guilt, sadness, love, gratitude, patriotism, and the list goes on. I have known a lot of emotions in the course of my life; some I wish I had not experienced so dramatically. But I do believe that not to show any emotion is unhealthy, and I believe that being healthy is critical to making a positive difference in life over the long haul. There was a time in my life when I was unabashedly crying with an overflow of emotions. It involved a young man who pursued his dreams. This young man had talent, and the competition was stiff to say the least! It was at the ceremony when your flight class marched into the auditorium, Air Force, Marines and Naval pilots together in the same class! The patriotic songs blaring, the pictures of all the various planes in service, the general speaking, and after all of this—the general hands you the wings. You take a few steps and turn around. You nod. I walk up and then you have me pin on your wings. Nothing, anywhere, anytime, will cause such emotion in my life. Then for you to receive the Airman's Award as the best pilot— what more can I say? I couldn't say a thing, so the dam broke and the tears came. Now you know why I believe in emotions. Over your lifetime you have brought out the best of them in me.

Love, Dad

Gratitude
March 30, 2009

Son,

If your pattern continues as it has been, then you are on another mission today.[48] It is impossible for me to fully comprehend the challenges and demands that you not only face but welcome as you fulfill your commitment to duty in service to our country. I know that the place you repeatedly fly into harbors the so-called training ground for those who wish to destroy the "infidels" of the West. I have a sense of pride in what you do and am confident that you are among the best trained of any in the world. I also have noticed that my level of awareness for our service men and women has exponentially increased because of you being where you are and doing what you do. The way I handle the aspect of uncertainty (not falling completely apart) is by a special focus. The key in this focus is gratitude, or what the Scriptures refer to as *thanksgiving.* Specifically gratitude for you, for your character, for the sense of calling you have, for your determination to be the very best you can be, for your centering, for your consistency, for your heart, for your having the balls to do what you do, and all the while being the gentle soul that you are. It is this focus of gratitude that enables me to have a peace that is all-encompassing. Never before have I understood the depth of meaning found in this familiar writing: "The Lord is near. Do not be anxious

---

48   Twenty-four hours on duty, flying missions of up to twenty-two consecutive hours; twenty-four hours off duty; twenty-four hours on, etc.

about anything, but in everything by prayer and petition with *thanksgiving*, present your requests to God. And the peace of God which transcends all understanding, will guard your hearts and your minds in Christ Jesus."[49] This is how I handle your flying into harm's way: with gratiude for who you are and what you do.

Love, Dad

---

49   Philippians 4:5b-7

The Night or the Light
April 16, 2009

Son,

Recently I listened again to Susan Boyle singing "I Dreamed a Dream." There are a lot of lines that stand out for me. One line is "but the tigers come at night." (Schonberg & Kretzmer, 2009) Over the years in my own life and in the lives of people I have seen as a therapist or life coach, I observed the truth of this refrain: the <u>nights</u> of doubt, the <u>nights</u> of disappointment, the <u>nights</u> of loneliness, the <u>nights</u> of what might have been, the <u>nights</u> of serious illness, the <u>nights</u> of loss. The metaphor is easily understood. It is at night that we cannot see clearly, cannot easily find our way, can more easily get off track, can change direction and wind up where we least expected or planned or hoped or dreamed. I don't think that it is by happenstance that a relationship with Christ is termed as "walking in the light." Light is the most revealing thing in the world. The dark days of Europe were revolutionized by the period commonly referred to as the period of En*light*enment. So often the basic disciplines of reflection, meditation and prayer are neglected in our busyness. Why is it that some people choose to walk in darkness rather than light, even though, as the line from *Les Miserables* states so clearly, all the "tigers" come at night? Growth depends on light. Health depends on light. Life depends on light. The choice is basically everyone's as to where they spend their time—in the night or in the Light.

Love, Dad

Believing in You
April 19, 2009

Son,

There is universal truth that what a person believes impacts their life in a pivotal way. If people believe that all things can potentially work together for good or some grand purpose, they usually can handle the vicissitudes of life. If people believe that they have been dealt a raw deal, then they often become cynical or angry. If people believe that they are better than others, then they can become arrogant or condescending. So belief is really important, even though there are some poorly brain-endowed individuals who claim that belief does not matter. One area of belief that is often overlooked is that we, as people, need someone to believe in us. You know that in my own early experience (of being kidnapped, etc.) I had no one that conveyed to me that kind of belief. The first inkling came when I received a scholarship to a prep school. However, that was simply a belief that I could play football, not necessarily a belief in me as a person. There was a man by the name of Glen Barker,[50] who, for some incredible reason, thought that I could make a difference. No one else up until that time had conveyed that to me in such a tangible manner. He created in me the hope of possibility. Decades later this same man passed from the earth. His children asked me to speak at his memorial service, just as he had asked me to speak at his wife's memorial service. He, without a doubt, enabled me to become who I have become. I am not finished *becoming* (as many, wistfully, would tell you!) but he was the kick start. I am aware that you know that from day one, I have always believed in you. You already have demonstrated your extraordinary abilities to this point in your career and personal life. I do believe that there are no limits to what you can do nor who you will become in terms of impacting others.

Love, Dad

---

50 Dr. Glen Barker was the Chairman of the Department of New Testament Studies at Gordon Conwell Divinity School. A brilliant theologian and a 'man among men', he was an avid competitor in multiple areas and served as the Basketball Coach of the seminary basketball team which recruited athletes to consider seminary grad school after they finished their college degree. He is the person who encouraged the author to study at the seminary while he (the author) served as the Baseball Coach at Gordon College following his graduation there. Barker served as his Academic and Spiritual Coach in seminary and was one of four professors who spoke at Paul's ordination service, giving the main address. Later Dr. Barker encouraged him to pursue his doctorate in Clinical Psychology at Fuller Graduate School after Dr. Barker had moved there to become the Dean of the Faculty. The author says that one of the highest honors he ever received while serving as a minister of the Gospel was when Dr. Barker asked him to speak at his own wife's memorial service.

Risk Is Part of Life

June 19, 2009

Son,

I was looking at your double wings[51] yesterday under the model of the C-17 you fly. I have not changed my mind about being adverse to the idea of jumping out of a perfectly capable airplane! However our eighty-five year old ex-president (George H.W. Bush) celebrated his birthday by doing exactly that! In reality, taking risks is part of living. If you cannot risk, you cannot grow. If you cannot grow, you cannot become your best. And if you cannot be your best, you cannot be fulfilled, and then what is life all about? Fulfillment, however, is never a goal; it is always a result—a result of purpose beyond one's self.

Love, Dad

---

51   Double wings is a patch awarded only to those pilots who have earned both flying and parachute wings.

Sister Hilda
July 9, 2009

Son,

Well, Charleston is really warm in July, but it's going to be warmer when you head back across the pond to the "sand box" next week. It's always relative when it comes to circumstances. Aren't you glad that you have learned "whatever, bring it on!" throughout your training! Attending Catholic school when I was a child was the only time I thought circumstances were everything; *at least that's what the nuns said!* Here were some of the circumstances that were considered deadly (mortal sins):

1. Slow dancing with chests touching,
2. Anything involving the tongue except licking ice cream or talking, and
3. Thinking about the first two!

These circumstances precipitated a meeting with Sister Hilda, who I sincerely believe was a former drill instructor at Parris Island or a CTA at Jack's Valley.[52] These memories (apart from Sister Hilda) taught me that with God's help I could handle any circumstance. The neat thing about you, Son, is you didn't

---

52   Jack's Valley is an area at the Air Force Academy known for basic training of new cadets during their doolie (first) year and their instructors are called Cadet Training Assistants.

need a Sister Hilda to teach you to depend on God's Presence, whether at 33,000 feet or on the ground. The Good Book has many promises; however, one of my favorites came from the lips of our Lord: "Lo, I am with you always, even to the end of the age."[53] I will pray especially that during these next 15 days this promise will give you great peace and confidence.

Love, Dad

---

53   Matthew 28:20b

Gift of Life
July 18, 2009

Son,

Today is another opportunity to experience growth in body, mind and soul by how we think and how we interact with our surroundings and with those with whom we socialize. It was twenty-eight years ago today that your mother was shot and the medical doctors told me that it did not appear that she would survive. Obviously, and thankfully, the prognosis was in error. It turned out, strangely enough, to be an event that allowed some growth choices to be made (like never taking anything or any person for granted, knowing that each day is precious). O. S. Marden (who, by the way, was raised in New Hampshire) said, "If you do not feel yourself growing in your work, and your life broadening and deepening, if your task is not a perpetual tonic to you, you have not found your place." (Marden, 1903) Marden did not have it easy while growing up. When he was three years old, his mother passed from this earthly scene, and when he was seven, his father died from injuries while working in the woods. Marden worked as a *hired boy*, persevered, and supported himself. Being motivated by a book he found in an attic, Marden set out to improve himself and wound up studying at Harvard and later at a theological seminary. He, along with others, believed that "the golden opportunity you are seeking is in yourself. It is not your environment; it is not luck or chance; it is in yourself alone." Sort of sounds like something a Carpenter once said: "The Kingdom of God is within you."[54]

Love, Dad

Mac and his mother

---

54   Luke 17:21

Response-Able
August 7, 2009

Son,

D wight David Eisenhower said, "The history of free men is never written by chance but by choice—their choice." (Eisenhower, 1956) As you work with people, you will often discover a mindset of being victimized or a culture of blame. You can hear this philosophy being expressed by certain politicians today. They have not discovered or discerned that fundamentally we are a product of choice. The realization of this great truth can excite one's sense of possibility, regardless of circumstances. It is perhaps the reason Victor Frankl wrote, "Say yes to life in spite of everything." (Frankl, 1959) It is an awareness of responsible as *response*-able. When it dawns on a person that choice is always a possibility, that insight is incredibly empowering!

Love, Dad

Effort and Reward
October 2, 2009

Son,

Tedy Bruschi, #54, one of the New England Patriots who recently retired, received the greatest compliment that Coach Belichick ever gave: "He was the perfect football player." (Chandler, 2009) Belichick is not known for speaking effusively about anything! At the retirement announcement, Bruschi said of Coach Belichick, "Yes, I knew how to play linebacker and I knew how to play. Parcells came in, Carroll came in, but I didn't know how to win until Bill came in here. He taught me how to win." (Bruschi, 2009) On a personal note, I did not grow up playing soccer, but I had a coach, Cliff McCrath, who is in more halls of fame than anyone else I know of. He is to soccer what Belichick is to professional football. Under his coaching, I actually did OK when I learned and played soccer in college.[55] There are some people who have the gift to bring out the best in others. I believe that officers in the Armed Services have the same responsibility to those under their command as coaches do to their players. The way that coaches do this is to never expect more of a player than what they themselves are willing to bring to their respective responsibilities. This is true of the Belichicks and the McCraths

---

[55] Under Coach McCrath, the author was MIP (most improved player), MVP (most valuable player) and Captain of his team all in the one season he played soccer in college.

and it is true of you! *There is a connection between effort and reward.* This is just one of the reasons our country is fortunate to have you as an officer in service as a member of the United States Air Force. You learned well to work your ass off!

Love, Dad

John Wooden
October 17, 2009

Son,

One of the pictures we have is that of John Wooden, who turned ninety-nine this week! Simply, he was the best college basketball coach ever. He was the principal speaker at the Basketball Hall of Fame induction ceremonies in Springfield, Massachusetts. He had been inducted as a player and a coach. His double induction is the only one in the Hall. Anyway, I was seated next to him during the ceremony and dinner, as I had given the opening prayer. It was an evening of meaningful conversation between us. A few weeks later he sent me a picture of himself with the following inscription: "'If God be for us, who can be against us? Commit your work unto the Lord, and then it will succeed.' Best Wishes, John Wooden UCLA." For Coach Wooden, it didn't make any difference what you did as a professional; the key was the manner and motive with which you were doing it! I know that this current assignment for you is one of supreme significance and that lives depend upon it. I can say nothing better than what Coach Wooden wrote to me those many years ago. I am confident you have made this commitment and that the results will have eternal significance.

Love, Dad

Veteran's Day

November 11, 2009

Son,

There are precious few days that combine solemnity and gratitude. Today, Veteran's Day, is one of these days. The voluntary response to "support and defend the Constitution of the Unites States against all enemies, foreign and domestic," in effect presupposes any price, anywhere, anytime, for as long as it takes. The price paid has been incalculable. Cemeteries like Aisne-Marne, Ardennes, Brittany, Flanders Field, Lorraine or Rhone all have rows of markers; they stand as silent sentinels guarding the honor and dignity of those who indeed gave their all. Before you even get to these silent sentinels in Margraten Cemetery, there is a wall with 1,772 names of those missing from the Army and the Air Force. The inscription cryptically reads, "These are those who sleep in unknown graves." The price these heroes paid is beyond measurement. Today, men and women like you, and your squadron mates, have answered the call to ensure that these who have given their all, have not done so in vain. May our Heavenly Father guide, strengthen and lead you with quiet confidence, and resolve, to victory after victory in our current war. And by His Grace, return you and your mates safely to a Grateful Nation.

Love and Gratitude, Dad

Christmas and the Heart
December 16, 2009

Son,

C hristmas. For some reason it causes me to think of people and experiences of past Christmases. It's not a mystery. Christmas is about heart—the heart of God and our hearts. Experiences of the heart are indelible. I know of no holiday that touches the heart like Christmas, for joy or for pain. I recall that while in college I had no home to return to for this great day, so I worked security for the school on Christmas Eve, checking the locks on the dorm doors—just a little lonely! Then of course there were Christmas Eve celebrations that were the other extreme. In a candlelight service, I had the privilege of speaking to several hundreds of people about the Babe who would one day be recognized as the King of Kings! In this service, with the sanctuary lit only by candles, a great tenor sang "O Holy Night." Whew! What an experience! The great experiences of life have always been those that not only touch the heart but imprint eternity! So this Christmas Eve will be one of these great experiences. Having the awareness that you will be deployed just a couple of days later to the Middle East, for the second time, causes thoughts and feelings that are immeasurable. Words cannot capture what I will be feeling. The place you have and will always have in my heart is peerless, not only by what you have done and will do, which is exceptional, but more importantly by virtue of who you are. Thus, this coming Christmas Eve, when I sit by the fire, will be one of those indelible experiences of Peace and Joy—the very message that the angels announced over two thousand years ago.

Love, Dad

Letter for Second Deployment
December 30, 2009

Son,

Today you leave the shores of the greatest country history has recorded, to fight a foe who embodies an ethic that dehumanizes man's dignity, the sacredness of life and the natural order; a foe who is sworn to destroy civilization as we have known it and to enslave people's minds in a manner that abrogates the rationality of humanity, with a resultant society of zombies who mindlessly go about slaughtering women and children. Men and women before you have answered the high calling and have paid the price it requires: loss of comfort, separation from loved ones, physical and psychological scars and, at times, their very lives. What they have gained is the loyalty and admiration of an *extended family*, one not of blood, but of shared values and mutual respect, brothers and sisters who have joined together in a righteous cause. The tradition of volunteerism began in this country with the War of Independence and has continued to this very day. You and your squadron mates, my son, embody all that is the best of the best, for you talk the talk and walk the walk. As you wrote to me last Christmas, before your first deployment, "in spirit we are inseparable."

With Love, Admiration and Pride, Dad.

To Dream a Dream
January 20, 2010

Son,

In the musical *Les Miserables*, there is one lyric that says, "Now life has killed the dream I dreamed." (Schonberg, Boublil, Natel, & Kretzmer, 1985) A comment on this very evocative line: many people don't have dreams of becoming anything. They just let life happen and then, down the road, sadly reflect on "what might have been." Often this is done in solitude, with close drinking buddies, a "shrink," an intimate friend or with God. Sometimes after reflection these people simply shrug and "go on" to live out what John Whittier wrote in these lines: "For all sad words of tongue or pen, / The saddest are these: 'It might have been!'" (Whittier, 1912) On the other hand, there are those who dare to dream and to undertake whatever their dreams require. One of the most important things a parent can do very early on is to give their children the encouragement to dream dreams, to have their child vividly imagine what would bring them great satisfaction, and then to encourage them to pursue those dreams. Along the way, the parent serves as a coach, a cheerleader and a friend. Sometimes unexpected detours open new vistas or perhaps close certain doors. How one responds to these circumstances can actually lead to incredible fulfillment, which would not have been known without these surprises. In my life I have known some of these detours. In retrospect and reflection, while we may be surprised, my confidence is that God is never taken by surprise. And to use a phrase with which you are familiar, with Him as "co-pilot" a person can confidently turn over the stick to Him, knowing that the forward journey is in good hands. I love the dreams you have dared to dream, wherever they may lead you.

Love, Dad

Freedom
February 5, 2010

Son,

In my practice I often hear people ask why they do the things they do. This is often asked with a sense that some outside influence or mysterious force is controlling them. Sometimes I want to remind them, with the words from Shakespeare's play, *Julius Caesar,* "Men at some time are masters of their fates. The fault, dear Brutus, is not in the stars, but in ourselves." (Julius Caesar (Act I, scene ii)) People in some sense may be temporarily restrained by the chains of fate— where they were born, who they have for parents, whether they are white, black, yellow, brown, Irish, Polish, English, Jewish, whatever! The chains are strong until people accept the gift of grace, which gives them the power of choice, thus enabling them to live with dignity *regardless of the hand that they are dealt.* This often frightens a person, for the realization that he or she has the power of choice is always accompanied by a sense of responsibility. This is more than they anticipated or desired. As the great Russian novelist Dostoevsky said, "Freedom is terrifying."[56] The reality is that a person pays for his choices. With this comes the realization that seeing oneself as a "victim" in life doesn't "play well in Peoria" or anywhere else!

---

56   The author is paraphrasing Dostoevsky's "The Grand Inquisitor" here, from The Brothers Karamazov.

Son, your pattern of choices demonstrates that your life is playing well *everywhere*, including Peoria!

Love, Dad

What Is True?
April 28, 2010

Son,

If something is true (real) versus false (delusional), it is real everywhere. Virtually every spiritual tradition teaches that your *higher* self is the presence of God within you. In Christianity, this inner knowing is said in this way: "The kingdom of God is within you."[57] In Confucianism we are told, "What the undeveloped man seeks is outside. What the advanced man seeks is within himself." In Buddhism we are reminded, "If you think the Law is outside yourself, you are not embracing the absolute Law but some inferior teaching." In Shintoism we are implored, "Do not search in the distant skies for God. In man's own heart is He found." And, finally, in Hinduism we are told, "God bides in the hearts of us all."[58] The critical question is, what does it take to get us to listen to this inner reality? Or what has caused us to grow deaf and calloused to its prompting? It is not complicated, but in our "busyness," this listening is challenging, to say the least. What it demands is for a person to be quiet. Easier said than done. Socrates' prayer is succinct and powerful: "Beloved Pan, and all ye other gods who haunt this place [earth], give me beauty in the

---

57   Luke 17:21 ASV

58   Overviews given by the author after researching various faith traditions for a lecture he was preparing to give for a local continuing education program called Adventures in Learning.

inward soul; and may the outward and the inward man be at one."
(Moore, 1922) The congruence of which Socrates was speaking is
realized by doing what the ancient prophet instructed all of us to
do: "Be still and know that I am God."[59] The awesome reality is
that in spite of the pace and demands of your professional career,
you have been cultivating the stillness required to possess this
oneness of which the ancient philosopher spoke. Well done, my
son.

Love, Dad

---

59   Psalm 46:10

What Kind of Father?

June 20, 2010

Son,

A special Sunday, "Father's Day!" When Christianity became personal to me, I loved the fact that people were taught by Jesus to address God as "Father" in what is known as the Lord's Prayer. "Our Father" is the beginning of perhaps the most widely known prayer in the world. The question, of course, is "what kind of Father?" Well, according to the teaching of Christ, the answer is not mysterious. He said to His disciples shortly before His death, "He who has seen Me has seen the Father."[60] In other words, the Father is approachable, not distant; affectionate, not cold; involved, not detached; loving, not calloused; supportive, not indifferent; faithful, not fickle; nurturing, not depleting; freeing, not controlling; intimate, not superficial or shallow. So on this Father's Day, my prayer for you is twofold: (1) that you will know God in all of these dimensions; and (2) that, as God the Father said of Jesus, you will have the same confidence that I say of you, "Behold my son, in whom I am well pleased"[61]—which, between you and me, is one hell of an understatement!

Love, Pride and Thanksgiving, Dad

---

60 John 14:9
61 Matthew 3:17

Transcendent Purpose and Optimism

August 10, 2010

Son,

S ometimes people can be fooled by what they think they know. Henry Ford had engineers who told him that their research proved "unbreakable glass" was impossible. Ford told his human resource people to hire some college kids who had not learned this "reality." Unbreakable glass was the result! I'm not as creative as Ford, but if penicillin can be made from moldy bread and fertilizer from horse s*#!, then I think there isn't much that can't be tried if one is resourceful and persistent. Helen Keller said it best: "No pessimist ever discovered the secret of the stars, or sailed to uncharted lands, or opened a new doorway for the human spirit." (Keller, 1903) Commitment to a transcendent purpose and optimism are a surefire way to make a difference.

Love, Dad

Stained Glass
August 13, 2010

Son,

E lisabeth Kubler-Ross said, "People are like stained-glass windows. They sparkle and shine when the sun is out, but when the darkness sets in, *their true beauty is revealed only if there is a light from within.*"[62] (Kubler-Ross, 2003) You have chosen to embrace in your "inner man," a light that no darkness can cover. Thousands of years bear testimony to people who have had this kind of light. They transcend circumstances and challenges. It's another "grand and noble tradition" in which you have taken your place.

Love, Dad

---

62   Emphasis is the author's.

Indomitable Spirit
August 17, 2010

Son,

All the wonders you may ever seek are already within you. Take time today (just a few minutes) to be quiet, and you will know this reality existentially. Man has never made any material as resilient as the human spirit. Your spirit is indomitable. The Buddha said, "In the confrontation of the stream and the rock, the stream always wins, not just by strength but through persistence."[63] The vital aspect for any of us is not what is behind or before, but what is within.

Love, Dad

---

63   This is commonly attributed to Buddhist teachings but may be mistakenly assigned to Buddha.

More Than Required

August 30, 2010

Son,

While in grad school, I played baseball for the town of Hamilton on the North Shore of Boston, Massachusetts. In exchange, I received housing on what was known as the Ayer Estate. Our home field was named Patton Park, named after the famous general. There was actually a Patton tank located in the distance next to the field! Many stories about Patton are well known. However, one of his sayings that is not well known is "Do more than is required of you." [commonly attributed] This is, of course, what separates the average from the extraordinary. There is nothing average about you.

Love, Dad

Alert Status
October 10, 2010

Son,

I never appreciated the word "training" until I began to seriously examine what some of our service men and women go through to be the best. You have made this idea come alive. This weekend you are on elevated alert status. In a matter of three weeks you will depart for your third deployment—prepared for a performance of excellence on every level, from airmanship to leadership, intellectually, physically and emotionally. With all that I have seen in my lifetime, not much puts me in awe or finds me at a loss for words, yet what you have done and are doing has that effect. The way I handle it is to embrace the words found in the ancient writings of the Jewish prophets Isaiah and Nehemiah. Isaiah wrote what he believed was the word of the Lord regarding His protection for His children: "Fear not, for I have redeemed you. I have called you by name, you are mine. When you pass through the waters, I will be with you, and through the rivers they shall not overwhelm you; when you walk through the fire you shall not be burned, and the flame will not consume you. For I am the Lord your God, the Holy One of Israel, your Savior."[64] And as is written elsewhere, it says Nehemiah "prayed and posted a

---

64   Isaiah 43:1-3a

guard."[65] Indeed, you are on alert this weekend—but you have been for a long, long time, and that is why I sleep well at night.

Love, Dad

---

65   Nehemiah 4:9

Song for the Journey
October 12, 2010

Son,

I t has been fourteen years that you have been putting up with
these "Thoughts for Today," or what may be called a beaten
track of habitual suggestion. The motivation for sending these
during all sorts of circumstances is my firm belief that sustaining
a particular thought because one chooses to, when one might have
other thoughts, is a vivid illustration of the freedom of individual
will. This exercise of thought has nothing to do with feeling good.
If merely feeling good could decide what was right and beneficial,
then drunkenness would be a superior state of being! Everything
we do or become or accomplish begins with our thought life. How
one sees oneself, or others, or the universe, begins within the arena
of the mind. The great challenge that the Master Teacher laid out
for those who listened was "after thought" (in Greek: *metanoia*),
to live in a special way—a way that uplifts! If individuals are
exceptional, they invariably live by an ideal springing up from
their mind's eye. Coherent thought then becomes a torch that
is inextinguishable. And then no circumstances of life can keep
the nightingale of peace and purpose from singing in their hearts
during the sacred journey of life. Added to all this stuff, my
motivation in sending these TFTs to you is basically my love and
gratitude for you.

Dad

Scholars and Warriors
October 15, 2010

Son,

I love the multifaceted life you are living—accepting challenges across the spectrum. You remind me of something I read a long time ago, written by one of my favorite Greek historians by the name of Thucydides. He lived about four hundred years before Christ was born. This is what he said: "The nation that makes a distinction between its scholars and its warriors will have its thinking done by cowards and its fighting done by fools." [commonly attributed] Because of you, and those few like you, our nation need not worry.

Love, Dad

Unselfish and Noble Actions

October 17, 2010

Son,

There are people, and as long as there are people, there will be all kinds of people—of all colors, all different lifestyles, all different values, all different likes and dislikes. There is one kind of person that demands respect, and there is another that commands respect. The latter does not seek attention or notoriety; they simply awaken each day to be the best they can be and to do the best they can do. These are the men and women of our all-volunteer military. David Thomas, a nineteenth century English writer, said, "Unselfish and noble acts are the most radiant epochs in the biography of souls." (Gilbert, 1895) I'm sure he would have written more, Captain, if he had met the men and women in the 16th Airlift Squadron as you all prepare to leave for another deployment.

Love, Dad

Awareness

October 24–25, 2010

Son,

Contrary to popular opinion, the Christian "worldview" never was meant to be a "religion." In fact, Jesus Himself had most of His difficulties with people who were very religious. Rather, the great emphasis from this Carpenter of Galilee was on a certain kind of *awareness*—awareness that the fully alive person was made for relationship—relationship with people, and relationship with everything in creation, and at the core of that person's being, a relationship with the Creator. This relationship would involve all dimensions of a person: their mind, their body, their emotions and their soul. In other words, *their all*. People who came to realize this were considered in those early days as people of *The Way*. This designation came about because this same Carpenter said very cogently that He was the Way.[66] People had thought that God was distant, that individuals didn't matter unless they all did things similarly to one another, whether it was the way they prayed, the way and what they ate, or the way they celebrated. By contrast, Jesus came and He touched the untouchable, cured the incurable, and loved the unlovable. In Scripture, He points to the lilies of the field, the birds of the air and draws implications of a benevolent Creator who desires to care, comfort and console

---

66   John 14:6

those who are ignorant of life's basics. He epitomizes the reality that Love is indeed what life and what God is all about and that this kind of *Love* is demonstrated in myriad ways: affection, affirmation, approachability, awareness and at times even anger. In the Bible, He goes fishing, He picnics, He parties, He talks, He listens, He prays, He teaches, He mingles, He withdraws and retreats for times of solitude and renewal. Religious? I don't think so. Awareness? Unquestionably! Having this awareness is the beginning of the greatest journey one can ever experience. It will be challenging and at times frustrating. Yet it will be a journey of light against darkness, and a journey without end, for time and eternity—and very significantly, a journey through which you will never be alone. There are people who study the lives of significant people in history and attempt to carry out their beliefs. These may be Marx or Freud, Aristotle or Plato, Augustine, Kepler or Newton, whoever. When it comes to the founder of the Christian's awareness, it's an entirely different matter, for what the New Testament makes clear is that the Christian experience is not one of "imitating Christ." It's not about reading His plans and then carrying them out; quite frankly, no one can do that task. It's about Christ being formed in us, and He then carries out the task. It's not about a good man who died two thousand years ago; it's a living Man still as much a man as you, and still as much God as when He created the world, really coming and really entering into your very self! God looks at you in the same way He looked at His Son, because His Son is in you, thus enabling "Sonship" to be your experience! As Scripture tells us, "And because you are a son, God has sent the Spirit of His Son into our hearts, crying 'Abba Father', no longer a slave but a son, and if a son, then an heir."[67] Christ will just not "accompany" you on this deployment like one of your co-pilots; He is 'within' you; He and you are One.[68] Read, study, memorize, meditate on this great text, for your life will never be the same with Him dwelling within you.

Love, Dad

67   Galatians 4:6-7
68   Galatians 2:20

Making a Difference
October 26, 2010

Son,

S ome people live an entire lifetime and wonder if they have ever made a difference in the world. The pilots of the 16th Airlift Squadron don't have that problem. In less than forty-eight hours you will leave for your third deployment. In the land to which you are going, you will be surrounded by the good, the bad and the ugly, yet you will prevail. You are a learning creature, and it makes no difference if you are learning a weapon, a system, a piano or a jet. What I have noticed about you reminds me of the champion wrestler I knew many years ago. We have in our library a piece of the Berlin Wall he gave to me when he returned from his European Tour. The key to his success was stated in an old martial arts saying: *the master is the one who is willing to stay on the mat longer every day than anyone else.* Throughout your career you have consistently "stayed on the mat" longer than was asked in order that you might become the best. It worked.

Love, Dad

The 15ᵗʰ Club
October 28, 2010

Son,

O ne of the books we have in the golfing section of our library
is titled *Your 15th Club*. It is a book by Bob Rotella and
emphasizes the importance of the mind in competitive golf.
According to the rules of golf, everyone can have fourteen clubs.
The difference is that champions have a fifteenth club! Not a
physical club, *but something more important than equipment*. Rotella
says that just as equipment, physical fitness and golf-swing
mechanics are important, the *mindset* is what distinguishes the
acceptable and the good from the best. He goes on to emphasize
that just as one is always checking physical equipment and
swing mechanics, one has to keep their mind in shape as well.
In summary, a mind will become weak, just as your body will, if
you don't continue to work it out. As your father, I am at peace
as you leave for the combat theater this morning, knowing your
"15th club" is the finest in your bag.

Love, Dad

Mac hugging his mother after deplaning at Pease AFB

Pease Send-Off
October 29, 2010

Son,

I cannot put into words my feelings when watching the welcome you and your squadron mates received at Pease Air Force Base yesterday.[69] (The interview on the TV with the three of us was on the Boston news on Channel 4 last evening. Obviously you were the star! I was impressed that you spoke and gave no specifics regarding details of what you would be doing or where you would be doing it!) The terrific aspect to all of this is a truism that so many people miss; to wit: when committed to a cause beyond one's self, one has an impact never anticipated. It was for me, as an observer more than a participant, a peak experience—not planned, not expected and not sought, yet incomparable and beyond words. According to Maslow, "People during and after peak-experiences characteristically feel lucky, fortunate, graced...In this context

---

69　As Mac and his squadron-mates were boarding the plane in Charleston for their transport to their deployment into harm's way abroad, he learned that they would be landing at Pease Air Force Base in New Hampshire to refuel. He told that to his father, who, along with Mac's mother, broke the speed limit to get to Pease prior to the transport plane. Pease has a contingent of volunteers who welcome every U.S. Air Force plane with troops deploying or returning from the field of conflict. It just so happened that this was the 200th greeting and so was celebrated in a special way. When Mac deplaned at Pease, he was surprised to see his parents in the front row to greet him.

we are accustomed to this sort of thing—that is, to the feeling of gratitude or all-embracing love for everybody and for everything... leading to an impulse to do something for the world, an eagerness to repay, and even a sense of obligation and dedication." (Maslow, 1994) Maslow was absolutely correct! Thank you for who you are, what you are doing and most importantly who you have become and are in the process of becoming. These six months at Falcon's Nest will not be the same until you return, but then, "Watch Out, World!"

Love, Dad

Thanksgiving
November 25, 2010

Son,

From a psychological and theological perspective, when a person stops being grateful, his or her thinking becomes fuzzy, hazy and befuddled. A grateful heart produces clear thinking. This is why Thanksgiving is not just a special day; it's the heartbeat that fosters strength, purpose, peace and humility. For many, thankfulness is dependent on circumstances; if so, it's a damn far cry from those pugnacious pilgrims who gathered for that first celebration. Those daredevils ardently believed, quietly dared, calmly endured, believed God and expected Him to do the impossible, and thus challenged the overwhelming odds. God had proven Himself in Jesus Christ and that was good enough for them. Happy indeed are the thankful ones who have not turned the cup of life upside down; they still dance and dream as those who believe that their work is God's work. I love the way you dance and dream! Happy Thanksgiving Captain, my Captain.

Love, Dad

Rebooting
December 1, 2010

Son,

I'm convinced that the fact some people act nicer as they get closer to Christmas is parallel to the way my computer works! Occasionally, I will get this message on my screen: "Server is not connected." What I do then is reboot the modem. Pretty basic and pretty easy. I think that playing Christmas carols in stores, on TV, in hospitals, clubs, just about all over, is actually helping people to metaphorically reboot, to check their connection to the "Server." Your rituals are your way of staying connected. As a result, the message from you and through you is always clear.

Love, Dad

Homeward Bound
March 2, 2011

Son,

Great to have you back in the States! Your own bed, shower, kitchen, your books, the gym on base, on and on! You were correct in quoting Scott: "Breathes there the man, with soul so dead, who never to himself hath said, 'This is my own, my native land!'" (Carman, 1904) The reception our men and women are receiving these days upon landing speaks volumes. Wish I could have been there as you got off the plane... Your friends will be glad you are back to rejoin your own squadron. Speaking of friends, Emerson said, "A friend may well be reckoned the masterpiece of nature." (Emerson, 1874) I will raise a toast to your friends when we are together.

Love, Dad

Eustress
March 4, 2011

Son,

I figure one of these days you will be contributing to the website *afterdeployment.org*. It has stuff you have been reading, experiencing and living for quite some time! Sound health-care providers know that *congruence* is a big deal in maintaining health. It appears that some returning vets, as well as professional and business people, and people in general, have a difficult time with this health principle. Some people have not learned that the worst thing you can do for your health is to deny, block or suppress emotions, whether good or bad. This makes a person extremely toxic. (You, I happily observe, don't follow this pattern.) There is, however, an antidote for this toxicity. It is gratitude. It changes stress into *eustress*, which energizes and invigorates! It is an antidote that is impossible to overdose on. With this in mind, choose to have a *growing and balanced* day.

Love, Dad

LOVE

2011- 2017ff

THE GREATEST OF
THESE IS LOVE

Hand-Me-Downs

March 19, 2011

Son,

Many of the things in our home are hand-me-downs. They are especially valuable because of what they symbolize, the stories behind them, the people who gave them, the circumstances surrounding them—all of the above. If hand-me-downs create stories that inspire energy that is positive, how good is that? Some people have "apartments" in their minds with "hand-me-down furniture" that, unfortunately, does just the opposite. It is tattered and the springs are broken; the legs are wobbly. Such furniture includes hand-me-down thoughts like "You really can't be an athlete because you're too skinny," or "You're not fast enough," or "You really are not smart enough to take college courses."[70] Many people become comfortable with mental hand-me-down furniture, which really needs to be replaced. Somebody asked me the other day what I did for work. I told them I was a programmer who specialized in good furniture, advising people when to go to the dump and bring in new stuff. Their response: "You're kidding!" I said, "The key is knowing how to make an assessment, where to shop and what the cost will be." It can be incredibly refreshing and satisfying. Fortunately, your hand-me-downs are terrific. In

---

70   These are comments the author remembers being made about him when he was growing up.

---

fact, they remind me of what the other Paul (the Apostle) said, "For I have delivered unto you what the Lord gave to me."[71]

Love, Dad

---

71   1 Corinthians 11:23

Commitment
April 2, 2011

Son,

Today will be a huge day in the life of your very special friend Jason. I'm happy for you that your schedule allows you to be in the wedding party. Marriage is all about the capacity of commitment. *Commitment enables you to get through the difficult times.* You learned this early on in your life, whether you were protecting the sheep, having an upper-class numb nut for a roommate at Cardigan your first year, facing the demands at Brooks, or dealing with upper-class members at the Academy your doolie year! Everyone has difficult times; Jason and his wife will have theirs. What he can draw upon is that he has demonstrated the capacity for commitment. It's just one of the reasons he, and you, are pilots. *Commitment enables a person to reach their goals*: no giving up, no turning back, no quitting. The key, of course, is to establish goals that cover the basics: physically, intellectually and spiritually. *Commitment enables you to keep your word.* Some people talk a lot but don't walk the walk. When a person has integrity, what they say comes to pass *if it is at all up to them*. With all this said, it's no surprise that you and Jason are not just classmates, but close friends as well. A man's friendships are the true measure of a man's wealth. You two are rich indeed!

Love, Dad

Exploration of the Life
June 3, 2011

Son,

I was listening to someone recently who grew up in an atmosphere of fear and survival. (Because of confidentiality, I won't mention his name.[72]) Fear and survival were the two dominating forces in his life. He said he learned to compensate by making choices that, for a brief time, allayed his fears and enabled him to function at a certain level. To the untrained eye, he appeared to be just another young man who tried hard but whose future wasn't too bright. He mentioned that he had made some good decisions, like always looking for jobs, any jobs—from dish washing, to delivering newspapers, whatever—it didn't matter. He mentioned other decisions he had made that, unfortunately, were hurtful and resulted in self-afflicted wounds, which were then followed by guilt, loneliness and feelings of inadequacy, not to mention acts that hurt others. He told me that as he grew older, looking for closeness, he found it easier to take off his clothes than to uncover his inner self. He went on to share that a time came when he realized that there was "a dimension within" to which he had not hitherto paid attention. He said he did not know what to call this dimension—perhaps his core, or his soul, or his vital

---

72   This "young man" is actually based on the author and his own personal background.

being, whatever. He realized that this center needed nourishment. Then he remembered something Kierkegaard mentioned, to wit, "Life can only be understood backwards, but must be lived forwards." I asked what had triggered this dramatic awakening. His reply was simply that he met someone who believed in him. That gift enabled him to see something in himself that alone he could not see. I am looking forward to spending more time with him and learning other things, which I will share with you.

Love, Dad

Shared Values, Shared Priorities
June 7, 2011

Son,

I was part of a commitment service this weekend. The ceremony was held because of the love between two individuals. Most people do not think of marriage in terms of the "heroic." I do. Heroism is based not just on feelings, which are like the tide, but on will, reason and values. Unselfishness is the reason why love lasts and the only reason it grows exponentially. It is glorious and profound in the sense that the giver of this kind of love becomes the recipient! Lao-Tzu and Confucius, Buddha, Moses and Hillel, and Saint Francis of Assisi are striking examples of this love. For some reason, which I have not as yet figured out, this kind of love is not normally associated with marriage. I ask, why not? It would appear that for many, tits and ass have replaced heart and soul. We live in a culture that is surface-oriented and, as a result, very shallow in its depth and strength. Unfortunately, shallow people don't know or understand what commitment is all about. It's all about shared values and, as a result, shared priorities, a *Weltanschauung* if you will. The cogency of your values and the clarity of your capacity of commitment enables me to have no anxiety about any relationship to which you will commit, because you understand what commitment means.

Love, Dad

Commitment of Character
June 8, 2011

Son,

Important things really aren't all that complicated. It's just that they require commitment. For example, character isn't a mystery; it is basically the sum total of all our everyday choices. The character we develop tomorrow will be the result of the choices we make today. It was the German philosopher Goethe who observed, "Talent can be cultivated in tranquility; character only in the rushing stream of life." (Maxwell, 2007) The reason is obvious, even to non-philosophers, for when "it" hits the fan, the depth of talent may falter but character will not. Being a clutch player is critical in all areas of life, ranging from relationships to professional responsibilities. Circumstances are out of our control; character is not. Nothing will influence your character as much as the important relationships in your life. As John Maxwell says, "Almost all our sorrows can be traced to relationships with the wrong people and our joys to relationships with the right people." (Maxwell, 2007) The most important relationship one can ever have is with Jesus Christ. To paraphrase Blaise Pascal, *to bet that God was in Christ and lose, is to lose nothing; to bet that God was not in Christ and to lose, is to lose everything*. This great wager is the foundation of character that stands the test of time. I have great admiration for the choices you have made.

Love, Dad

Love
June 11, 2011

Son,

I have often heard the expression, "I fell in love." I want to ask, is it comparable to "falling out of a tree," or "tripping over a stone in the road?" I think the deal is really this: "I was attracted to her or him and we started to communicate." (Granted some people are better at doing this than others.) Communication can be on different levels, or at different tempos, but communication, per se, is *always critical*. It can be verbal; it can be made by facial expressions, a look; or it can be expressed by actions and deeds, or even by silence! But "falling"? I don't think so. Falling suggests being out of control or having an outside force like gravity taking over! By contrast, *love is a choice*. Many people don't make the decision to give it, because they are not sure of the return. They fail to realize that in giving, they in actuality receive. They don't understand that the decision to love is up to them; it's not a bloody virus! Now as a "shrink," I freely admit that some appear to be much easier to love than others, but ease is not what love is all about; love is the fulfillment of having a closeness and support that is encouraging, empowering, exciting and enabling, in order to become what one could never become in isolation. The choice, in some ways, is a trifle daunting, but the consequences of commitment can bring inestimable joy and immeasurable self-understanding and personal peace. The choices are twofold: (1) how does one want to give love? and (2) what kind of love does one wish to receive? Like many other things, it's all about choice.

Love, Dad

Miracles of Grace
July 19, 2011

Son,

Yesterday was the thirtieth anniversary of the moment an emergency-room surgeon told me to make phone calls because he didn't feel your mother would survive the point-blank shooting inflicted upon her by two robbers. Miraculously, she survived. Seventy-four years ago I was kidnapped at the age of eight months, going from infancy to young adulthood without a mother's tenderness or a father's guidance and encouragement. The inner city of Bridgeport, Connecticut, one may conclude, was not the most nurturing environment. There are indeed all sorts of miracles—some very dramatic, some not. Yet today your mother and I feel incredibly blessed and know indeed "all things can work together for good."[73] We are the beneficiaries of a profound Grace-consciousness for two very different reasons. The fact that the both of us, from ridiculously opposite backgrounds, have a son like you is testimony to the fact that the miracle-working power of our Lord is limitless. Your mom and I survived, and I do believe people would have given neither of us much of a chance given the rather catastrophic events that happened to us both many, many years ago. There is a testimony written thousands of years ago which says, "I will say of the Lord, He is my refuge and my

---

73   Paraphrase of Romans 8:28

fortress, my God in whom I trust . . . His faithfulness will be your shield."[74] This is a truth your mom and I have experienced, and we claim it for you today and all of the years that lie before you and yours.

Love, Dad

---

74   Psalm 91:2, 4b

Hope, Prayer and Healing
July 20, 2011

Son,

With everything going on with your grandparents medically these days,[75] it reminds me of the importance of the attitude of both the patient and their doctor when it comes to healing. The impact of studying placebos has shown how important a role belief plays in the recovery process. The effects of suggestion are well known. (A question that is sometimes asked is, "Does my doctor make me feel better or worse when I'm around him or her?") The power of a physician's belief system to shape the patient's response to therapy is akin to prayer. Both prayer and belief are nonlocal manifestations of consciousness, because both can operate at a distance, sometimes even outside the patient's awareness. The key in all of this medical stuff is the same as in all of life: to wit, never obstruct healing or life by being unnecessarily pessimistic. Hope and prayer are obviously powerful, or they would not be such a universal expression of man's heart and mind. It was the ancient Pythagoras (mathematician and philosopher who lived around 550 BC) who said, "The most divine art is that of healing. And if the healing art is most divine, it must occupy itself with the soul as well as with the body, for no creature can

---

75   Nine months earlier, during Mac's last deployment, his grandfather had been diagnosed with late-stage pancreatic cancer, and at this time his grandmother was also being treated for a life-threatening illness.

be sound so long as the higher part in it is sickly." (Mead, 1901) So, my son, hope and prayer are mighty instruments that we all have at our disposal.

Love, Dad

Dealing with Grief and Loss

September 6, 2011

Son,

Yesterday was one of those days one cannot prepare for, not with all the experience, training and life itself, in terms of being there. I was asked to meet with a family whose son (fifteen years old) was killed in a fall from a hiking trail. *The way of dealing with loss and grief is as unique and singular as people themselves.* As a therapist in these moments, I find that the key to grief counseling is to say nothing that is canned or rehearsed, *for that which is critical above all else is the capacity to listen with the third ear.* When I am invited into a family's life during this particular time, a sense of sacredness dominates. Life for us all is about stages: they can be joyful or painful; peaceful or scary; growth or regressive; new or old; known or unknown. Life is all of these and more. We do understand this on a cognitive level, but to experience it existentially is where our dignity, as human beings, is the issue. It is a time when the character of heroism is revealed. It is the attitude that a person chooses in such circumstances that will, in a significant way, determine their future. A person's freedom is to take a stand on whatever conditions might confront him. Freedom is a spiritual capacity that only human beings possess, and thus *it is only human beings who can experience self-transcendence.* It is this truth that I pray will become very real, in the days ahead, for this young man's family.

Love, Dad

Unfolding in Relationships
November 4, 2011

Son,

Most people develop relationships eagerly, hoping to discover as much as they can about the other person. The unfolding reality, often to their surprise, is that they discover a far greater depth of knowledge about themselves! They discover what causes them to be happy, sad or frustrated. They discover what really is important in terms of a good night's sleep! They discover how much they actually don't know or understand! They discover how important quality listening is for closeness to occur. They discover that working together usually accomplishes a lot more than working alone. Relationships also serve as a great mirror, revealing what a person values. Letting relationships unfold over time is a glorious experience if the people in the relationships are each eager to become all that they can be and encourage one another to do the same. Speaking of relationships, the Master Teacher did *not* come to establish a new religion but, as you are aware, to invite people to experience a life changing relationship. I admire what I see in the relationships you have.

Love, Dad

Significance of Relationships
November 10, 2011

Son,

Relationships: the key to being fulfilled, the key to being all we can be, the key to being fully human and fully alive, the key to having an impact that is lasting, the key to growth, the key to inner peace, the key to being able to laugh at ourselves, the key to encouragement, the key to support, the key to endurance . . . Are you getting the idea that I think relationships are significant? Well, in fact, they are the most important reality in our entire lives—more important than things, more important than fame, more important than convenience or ease! Relationships can be verbal, cognitive, intellectual, emotional, spiritual, physical or social—or, if you are exceedingly blessed, they can be all of these. Some will be forever; some will be temporary. They may be romantic or platonic. The bonding may be based on common interest, common beliefs, common allegiances or common causes. The choices made in relationships will be a person's statement as to what he values. As such, it will be revealing as to his character—to wit, who he really is—and as such, will be eternal. I do believe it is one of the reasons that the Good Book says, "as we run the race before us, we are surrounded by a great cloud of witnesses who have also run the race."[76] These—our friends, our loved ones—are

---

76 Hebrews 12:1 (paraphrased)

now rooting for us, cheering us on in our race, and delighting in the special relationships we had and *continue to have with them*. And this constancy is reflective, my son, of the relationship we have and will have forever.

Love, Dad

Father and Son

Dropping the Fig Leaf
November 18, 2011

Son,

We are seeing that one of the aspects involved in running for office is that one's opponents or the press or just the morbid curiosity seekers will try to uncover secrets, past blunders, honest mistakes, etc., to make themselves look better. Ever since the beginning of recorded time, men and women knew by their nature that "fig leaves" were a part of the human experience. Most of the time, such fig leaves are worn to avoid being exposed to the view of others. This is unfortunate and yet understandable. Our private lives, of course, are designed to be private. No one should act like a schizophrenic nudist, indiscriminately letting everything hang out. On the other hand, the dangerous aspect of our fig leaves is that they can be used by the person themselves to hide not only from others but from themselves, as in areas of inadequacy, guilt or regrets. One's job, or one's past and present accomplishments, or one's title, or one's reputation can be used as a fig leaf. For example, during a period in my life, I used the little athletic ability I had to hide the fact that I was lonely, with no family and no assurance of things ever changing. I never had shared these facts with anyone. In some ways this fig leaf served me well in providing an opportunity to go to school without exposing my fear of never having any significant relationships. During the summer preceding my senior year in college, I allowed the fig leaf aspect of my athletics to be dropped. An amazing thing happened. I had the best year of athletics of my scholastic life. The freedom resulted in an empowering (as it always does). What was it that caused me to drop the leaf? Not complicated: it was simply Grace and the understanding of what Grace is all about and the acceptance that the future *could be as bright as the promises of God*. Now the implication of this understanding has happened to others for over two thousand years. It was the motivation behind the former slave trader John Newton to write his great hymn "Amazing Grace." It was his testimony that no longer was he hiding behind his fig leaf. It is the key that has enabled millions to look at themselves and to the Lord and say in freedom, "Here I am Lord; use me."

Love, Dad

(P.S. In case you were wondering, I could never run for political office.)

Inner Peace

December 1, 2011

Son,

From time to time I hear the statement "I don't know what I ought to do." It may be said about a relationship, a career, a move, a living arrangement change, whatever. What the years have taught me is that the best way for a person to discover what he ought to *do* is to find out who and what he *is*, for the path one embarks upon and the choices one makes is critical to who one is. The more a man knows about his own nature, dreams, temperament, ethics and values, the clearer the path becomes. There is a core within every person that distinguishes him from others while simultaneously identifying him with others. As John Greenleaf Whittier wrote, *"For of all sad words of tongue or pen, The saddest are these, 'It might have been.'"* (Lounsbury, 1912) Some people have a knack for growth evasion (a Jonah complex). The problem with this complex is that we all have a natural impulse to improve ourselves. When we don't, *we seed a deep inner conflict between who we were meant to be and who we actually are.* The problem is that we sense the divide, and restlessness is the result. Sometimes the restlessness remains beneath the surface (unconscious); at other times it's obvious to ourselves and to others. I love the insight of Saint Augustine, who, after being a priest for eight years, wrote, "For thou hast made us for Thyself, and our hearts are restless till they rest in Thee." (Augustine, 1943) The rest our hearts desire propels us forward with a peace that we are doing what we ought to do and at the same time becoming who we were meant to be. How good for me to know you have this peace.

Love, Dad

Trust

December 6, 2011

Son,

As you know, pilots have to trust their instruments; partners, one another; followers, their leaders; patients, their doctors; and people in general need to trust themselves. The first Christmas offers a lot of trust examples: the Wise Men who followed the Star, the shepherds who heard the angelic messengers, not to mention the trust between Mary and Joseph—wow, you've got to be kidding me! What is it about trust that is so paramount and crucial in all of life? Very simply, *without trust one cannot live freely, love deeply or have inner peace.* The glory of deep relationships is not a handshake or a pat on the back or a friendly smile. The riches of friendship are the spiritual inspiration that one receives because another trusts and believes in you. One of the statements of Jesus often overlooked by many is something he said to the disciples: "You are my friends."[77] This kind of friendship is experienced when you can think of a person and say to yourself or to that person, "I would trust him with my life." And so it is with you.

Love, Dad

---

77   John 15:14

No Excuses
January 11, 2012

Son,

66 Seek and you will find", "knock and it shall be opened"[78] are expressions many know, some believe, some doubt, and some interpret in their own way. When referring to these quotes in the Bible, we need to remember the context is that Jesus is talking to people about God. (Of course, if people read the whole story, they would be able to relax, for the bottom line is that God is seeking us.) But moving beyond the metaphysical world for a moment, the tantalizing "seek and you will find" is true in many areas. Looking for something to be upset about is not a problem; watch the news. By contrast, people who make a habit of seeking good usually find happiness, friendship, love, success, peace of mind. People who make a habit of seeking the negative usually find drama, hardship, setbacks and sorrow. The basic premise we all need to follow is "lose the excuses." One of the things I've noticed about you, which is quite rare, is that you don't make excuses. Keep living with this attitude and "the sky is the limit." Pun is intended.

Love, Dad

---

78   Matthew 7:7

Whole Relationships
February 9, 2012

Son,

Having seen numberless people over the years, I am convinced that George Bernard Shaw's play *Too True to Be Good* hit a bull's eye with his analysis that "bad" or "self-serving" behavior always comes back to haunt a person: "When men and women 'use' one another for their 'fun,' they get more than they bargained for because *men and women have a top story as well as a ground floor.*" (Shaw, 1961) When people partition up a person and see or use that person one-dimensionally, they are inviting big problems. The "hookup" philosophy of interpersonal relationships doesn't make it, because it's based on a fragmented view of humanity. I respect so very much the wholeness with which you have always viewed people, from the ground floor to the rooftop.

Love, Dad

Shit Happens

February 27, 2012

Son,

I've noticed that when a farmer sees a bumper sticker with the words "Shit Happens," he actually utters a prayer of thanksgiving! He knows that because of this truth, the corn crop, the tomatoes, the rest of his vegetables, etc., will all be better as a result of his collecting the manure from his cattle, horses and sheep and spreading it around. Farmers have learned that this stuff can be used in a profitable way. I know that when in the course of life "it happens," all too often people get bent out of shape. At that time I tell them to think like a farmer. They look at me rather askance until I explain two truths. Number (1) it does happen; and (2) they can use it to grow a healthier product. Most times the better product will be one's self. The experience can be used to clarify values, to better understand one's self and to establish future goals. So the word for today is "Think like a farmer when shit happens."

Love, Dad

Paralysis of Body, Not Mind
March 17, 2012

Son,

I remember being in Pakistan, meeting with an American who was crippled from some form of paralysis. He was on an "around the world" journey in a wheelchair! And he was getting a kick out of his journey! Nothing seemed to get him down. I asked him how he stayed "up?" His reply, which I never forgot, was "It's only my body that's paralyzed, not my mind." I have discovered, my son, that the paralysis of the mind is far more limiting than the paralysis of the body. The revitalized mind that is energized comes to grips with whatever lies before it. The neat thing about you is that your mind comes to grips with challenges, whatever they are. There was a tentmaker who also did exactly this. His words come ringing down through the ages: "I can do all things through Christ who strengthens me!"[79]

Love, Dad

---

79   Philippians 4:13

Love Cures
March 23, 2012

Son,

Early on, while pursuing doctoral studies in psychology, I studied the teachings of Karl Menninger. He taught that "Love cures; it cures those who give it and those who receive it." Sigmund Freud's definition of mental and emotional health was *the capacity to work and to love.* Love is tough as well as tender. One of the qualities of genuine love is intimacy—not just physical intimacy, but emotional, spiritual and cognitive intimacy as well; the sharing of not only an erection and breasts but fears, dreams and hopes on every level. Therein is a love which, when combined with commitment, is indeed empowering and transformational. Perfection resides only in the Godhead. We are always in the process of becoming. The right partner is the one who patiently draws all this out, believing that the other person is worth whatever time it takes. All one can deservedly expect is that each person will do their best. I see that you have always done your best. It makes me feel confident that your future is as bright as the promises of God on every level, both professionally and personally.

Love, Dad

Every Encounter Holy
April 23, 2012

Son,

Every relationship we have can be *holy* in the sense that we can choose to view everyone as evidence of God's creation. I grant that sometimes this viewpoint requires "thinking like a farmer,"[80] but the possibility of holiness is a reality. It all begins with intention. For instance, when you pass through a tollgate, the attendant can be viewed as a robot-like taker of the toll money or as a person who is willing to work, to earn an income and to be on the job regardless of weather or time. In addition, the awareness that a person—whether a tollgate operator, security guard, waitress, or maintenance personnel—is in fact a soul who needs to give and receive love and affirmation sends a nonverbalized message that is impossible to ignore. Treating the event, however brief, as a holy encounter creates an "attractor" energy. Viewing people in this way is a key in changing the ordinary to extraordinary. I am confident that today, in this sense, will be an extraordinary day for you.

Love, Dad

---

80   See TFT for February 27, 2012, "Shit Happens" (see page 197)

Things That Last
April 24, 2012

Son,

Time changes everything—that is, everything that is temporal. *Things that last (that are everlasting) are not subservient to time or circumstances.* Unfortunately, "forever" is a word often used by people who have not thought through the implications of its meaning. Early in my life I was one of those people. My awakening to reality had nothing to do with a course I had taken or an etymological word search. It had everything to do with your mom being shot three weeks after we were married and the doctor on duty informing me that her condition was critical and not looking good. She was partially paralyzed (which, as you know, she overcame), and she became very cautious, very security-conscious. The carefree "meet-me-anywhere" gal had understandably disappeared. One morning, when realizing how our life was about to change on every level, I looked into the mirror and said, "What are you made of, Paul MacVittie? You made a commitment that this was a *forever* relationship." It was an "Aha!" moment. Time did change everything since that day of her shooting, everything that was transitory. It did not change the forever commitment your mother and I made to one another because it was indeed a commitment of love. If, as the Scriptures teach, God is Love and we are made in His image and likeness, then the core of a person is not temporal. Thus, the reality of your mother's essence, of your essence and mine, was designed by the One who is the same yesterday, today and forever. When we genuinely love, it is deigned to be forever. It does not get better than this. The key is to never forget it.

Love, Dad

Be a Dreamer
June 8, 2012

Son,

I'm a big Norman Cousins fan. He wrote a lot of good stuff like, *Anatomy of an Illness,* which was a best seller, and for good reason! For me, one of his best statements can be summed up as "Death is not the greatest loss in life. The greatest loss is what dies within us while we live." I believe this, because to lose a dream is to lose that which keeps us going! Even one of our founding fathers, Benjamin Franklin, said, "Most men die from the neck up at age twenty-five because they stop dreaming." [commonly attributed] Perhaps one of the greatest assets people can have is to dream—to dream of making a difference in the world in which they live; to dream of being the kind of father or mother whose children will know they are loved and secure; to dream of being able to take a stand on principle rather than popularity; to dream of living up to one's potential; to dream of love that lasts, laughter that is healthy, work that is meaningful and a mind that is dynamic and expanding. These are the kinds of dreams that not only generate personal wellbeing but also impact the world in an immeasurable way. It is this kind of dreamer who is healthy. As a shrink and as a father, I am thankful that I can say my son is a dreamer.

Love, Dad

Getting Unstuck
June 28, 2012

Son,

I admire people who refuse to allow circumstances to get them stuck. Charles Krauthammer is a hero in this regard. He was paralyzed from the waist down from a diving accident while a medical student at Harvard. Rather than getting depressed or getting stuck or saying, "Why me, *God*," he completed his training, became a psychiatrist before becoming one of the most respected social/political writers or thinkers of this day. He's a happily married man with a son, a family who loves him and colleagues who respect him. By contrast, some patients I have seen over the years use the phrase that they are stuck. I ask them for a definition of "stuck" and their responses vary. It usually means they are emotionally down and they can't get up; they are not getting ahead in their job; or their relationship is not getting any deeper. What they don't understand is that the only people who get "stuck" are those who are stuck in their minds. The way to get a mind unstuck is the same way to get anything unstuck. It may involve a basic cleaning, as in any piece of equipment; it may mean that their power source needs to be plugged in; or they may be in a rut of their own making. Some car manufacturers make it very clear that certain engines run best on high-octane fuel. The car comes with all sorts of warnings that if you put low grade fuel in your tank, you will not get the same power or performance that you would if you were using high-test fuel. *The same is true in life.* If people just put junk into the engine of their minds, they are going to get stuck. These people need to see a shrink who is as practical as an automobile mechanic or engineer. It's not all that complicated. Lawyers and shrinks are notorious at making things complicated (that's how they can make more money!). Basically, people who get stuck need an engine overhaul. One of the reasons you don't get stuck is because of your daily "engine" checkups. Stick to the high-test fuel!

Love, Dad

Gratitude Is Riches

January 1, 2013

Son,

My prayer as we begin a new year is one of thanksgiving. I have learned that gratitude is riches and complaining is poverty. Cicero said something which many would do themselves good to focus upon: "If you have a garden and a library, you have everything you need." (Cicero, n.d.) Being able to feed both mind and body is in fact being wealthy and healthy. The simple things are those that paradoxically have the most depth. The year ahead holds opportunity for all of us to love, labor, laugh and learn. What more can we ask for? Nothing more.

Love, Dad

Wedding Toast
March 17, 2013

Son,

Whate a terrific day we all had in celebrating your marriage to Amanda. The toast I gave was based on my experience as a clinician as well as a husband. I will repeat it here as your first TFT in your married life: "The seismic paradigm change you experienced just hours ago will be understood in very practical and philosophical ways. Your world will go from *I* to *We*; from *Mine* to *Ours*; yet, paradoxically, your individuality will only be enhanced. The reason is basic. One can only fully develop

to one's unique potential in the context of love, for freedom to express one's self demands a love that encourages vulnerability to authenticity. We who are here pledge to you both our love and support as you begin this journey." I wanted you to be reminded of this toast and the exciting change that growth guarantees. I have seen a lot of change and hopefully growth in my own life over the years in many different areas. I even have purchased a sign to place near the bar in our family room that clearly illustrates inevitable change. It reads, "I've Reached the Age Where 'Happy Hour' Is Taking a Nap."

Love, Now and Forever, Dad

Definition of Freedom
March 20, 2013

Son,

O ne of the great themes of literature, whether it's in philosophy, psychology or theology, is that of freedom. Someone asked me to define it and out came "Freedom is man's capacity to take a hand in his own development, regardless of circumstances. It is our capacity to mold ourselves." Isn't it great to be free?

Love, Now and Forever, Dad

Mop Bucket Attitude

June 17, 2013

Son,

D ave Thomas, the founder of Wendy's Restaurants, told people he had his MBA. Of course, they all thought he was referring to a master's in business administration. What he actually meant by this acronym was a "mop bucket attitude." He would go on to say that this attitude was key in being successful, for all great leaders are willing to do *whatever is necessary* to lead a successful operation. Long hours? No problem. Incessant positive attitude? No problem. Constant improvement? Of course. Eagerness to listen? Absolutely. This kind of MBA is a great degree. Where's the "bucket" to be found? It's in every "room" of one's life.

Love, Now and Forever, Dad

Simply Do One's Best
July 30, 2013

Son,

Another day, another opportunity for fulfillment. It takes a while for many to understand that fulfillment is a result, not a goal. One of the things you learn in playing team sports is that the greatest satisfaction is often the side effect of one's personal goal to serve a cause greater than oneself—for a team's success or a company's success, or in service to a particular calling. The way this understanding becomes embedded is by listening to what your instincts, conscience and training command you. Success usually follows those who don't seek it; rather, they simply seek to do the best they can, wherever and whenever the opportunities present themselves. It's a principle that has stood the test of time. Today is such a day.

Love, Now and Forever, Dad

Vision versus Sight

August 1, 2013

Son,

Helen Keller said, "The most pathetic person in the world is someone who has sight, but has no vision." (commonly attributed) Along the same lines, Proverbs 29:18 says, "Where there is no vision, the people perish." This is true of any relationship, any organization, any business or anything that is alive, which of course includes each and every person. These are questions for everyone: What are my growth opportunities for this day? What can I do to understand more? What can I do to contribute more? How can I listen in such a way that I am able to distinguish between what is being verbalized and what is being said? Pressure is not always a bad thing. Self-imposed pressure to be all we can be provides a dynamic, invigorating energy that enables dreams to become a reality, which, in turn, fills our hearts with gratitude. There is nothing more edifying or magnetic than a grateful person who puts his work clothes on.

Love, Now and Forever, Dad

Purpose of these Thoughts for Today
March 21, 2014

Son,

Why the Thoughts for Today for all these years? Well, there are several reasons. The obvious one is that home is not a house where one lives, but it is *the relatedness in which one lives.* This relatedness remains dynamic regardless of geography. The rituals of taking time to listen and to touch form a connection that is eternal. In a strategic sense, these TFTs keep up the touching and the listening, and this is, of course, what rituals are meant to do. In ancient times, every social occasion had its rituals, from the greeting, the interaction and the dining, to the farewells. Patterns are a part of life, and from these patterns we learn a great deal. As an example, prayer and special music at bedtime were a norm for you. When a young person knows that they are listened to and touched, there is communicated to that individual the awareness that they are valued and prized. The end result of this is that in adulthood they function, in all interpersonal areas, out of a surplus rather than a deficit. One of the main assets of having rituals is the energy and strength that can be gathered from them. Holding hands around the table during a prayer of thanks is a perfect example. My prayer is that the ritual of these TFTs, through these many years, have served in some way to underscore the relatedness we have and thus undergird the truth that wherever you are, you are at *home* with us, and we with you. This awareness certainly gives me an energy and a trunkload of gratitude which reinforce the purpose to keep on keeping on.

Love Always, Dad

Cultivating Gratitude

August 27, 2014

Son,

Cultivating gratitude is among the most powerful and transforming spiritual practices in which one can engage. The power of gratitude is awesome. It can turn whatever we have into enough; it can take a simple meal and turn it into a feast. It is the key to living a life of nobility, enriching those with whom we interact. Authentic nobility is not inherited; it is generated from a thankful and humble heart that appreciates the sacrifices made by those who perhaps were and remain unknown. What we have, what we accomplish, what we enjoy is built upon the foundation of gratitude, which compels us to follow in the train of others who, by their lives, have inspired us to achieve. It is developed by opening our eyes and ears to sunrises and sunsets, to the beautiful music of a starlit night, and the morning cacophony of a chorus of wild, multicolored birds on the wing, soaring around a beautiful array of spectacular flowers. Taking time to recognize and reflect on all of these things, and more, will fill us with the incredibly transformative power known as gratitude. Today is not just another day, for today welcomes us to become what we have never been. It is a gift from the Creator of all that has been or ever will be to this moment. The Good Book says it simply and plainly: "This is the day the Lord has made; I will rejoice and be glad in it."[81]

Love, Always, Dad

---

81   Psalm 118:24 RSV

Attitude Quotient
November 6, 2014

Son,

It's a given that people with a high IQ have the potential to do some extraordinary things and, actually, some of them do. An intelligence quota can be an invaluable asset. However, what has also been observed is that something is even more important than IQ for making a significant difference in one's life, and that is what I would call an "AQ" rather than an IQ. What I mean by this is "attitude quotient." A productive person is not a person in a set of particular circumstances but a person with a particular attitude in any circumstance. What many people don't realize is that attitude is basically a decision. It's a decision that every day, every hour, every minute, we can determine what our attitude will be. A pessimist will look at a stone in his path as a stumbling block; an optimist sees the same obstacle as a stepping stone. Pretty basic, but so is life. Thomas Jefferson is said to have written, "Nothing can stop a man with the right attitude and nothing can help the man with the wrong attitude." It is clear that, because of your attitude, "through Christ all things are possible"[82]—your future, for you and those whom you love, is as bright as everlasting light. Enjoy the journey because you have embarked upon one in which you will never be alone.

Love, Always, Dad

---

82   Philippians 4:13

Never Alone

November 8, 2014

Son,

M other Teresa once wrote, "The most terrible poverty is
loneliness, and the feeling of being unloved." (Mother
Theresa Quotes, n.d.) Because of my crazy childhood (being
kidnapped, etc.), I completely agree with her. Hearing the sirens
going off during the Second World War while being alone is still
vivid in my memory. Years later, when I was a student in college,
everyone else had gone someplace for Christmas. I had no place to
go, so I earned money by being a watchman on campus, checking
the locks on the various buildings! My athletic teammates became
my family and, of course, the coaches cared on certain levels about
my well-being. Years passed, relationships came and went, and
all left an imprint of some kind. Yet in spite of this, or perhaps
because of all this, I became interested in the life of Jesus Christ.
It had nothing to do with religion, and those who know me at
this time in my life know I definitely am *not* religious. The more
I studied this historical Jesus, the more I discovered that His
teachings and life were all about the one thing I never knew, a
lasting relationship. The relationship of which He spoke was
with people, nature and the Source of everything that is, namely
God. I started to read and read and read even more, talk with and
listen to people, study history, psychology and every discipline
that dealt with humanity and why people did what they did and
lived like they lived. During these decades of learning, including
times of understanding, times of confusion, times of laughter and

times of tears, it became clear that I would never live long enough to have all my questions answered. However, there is something which I believe everyone desires and that desire can be summed up in one word: *assurance*—assurance that we matter, that we are loved, that we can contribute and make a difference in a positive manner and, finally, that we will never, never be alone. There is one testimony of this assurance that has buoyed me up through the years in the midst of painful and powerful events, celebrations of great blessings, as when you splashed down,[83] and the sundry aspects to all of life. It was the words of one who took a stand. It wasn't a Cicero or a William James, Kant, Hume, Fromm, Nietzsche, Socrates or Plato; it was a classic writer by the name of Isaiah (760 BC). This is what he said about God that we can all believe and never doubt: "But now says the Lord, who created you, He who formed you, 'Fear not for I have redeemed you, I have called you by name, you are mine. When you pass through the waters, I will be with you; and through the rivers, they will not overwhelm you; when you walk through the fire, the flame will not consume you. For I am the Lord your God, your Savior.'"[84] Having grown up in a world where, for me, there was no constant of love or companionship, this teaching provided for me a reason to be and to become. I want to reassure you of an eternal love that you have from me and, even better, from the God of eternity, who is with you at this very moment as you are completing this reading.

Love, Always, Dad

---

83   After Mac was born and the umbilical cord cut, when the author held him up to count his toes, Mac urinated in his father's face—thereafter, his birth was referred to as "splashdown."

84   Isaiah 43:1-3

Always Room for Growth

November 9, 2014

Son,

During the rather multifaceted professional career I have enjoyed over the years, I have learned some basic principles. First, it's not what you do that defines you but *what you bring* to what you do. Second, and tethered to this first principle, is the following: if you want to go fast, go alone; if you want to go far, go together.I recall speaking to a management team of top executives and asking them to introduce themselves to me as we went around the table. Every one of them told me their title and what they did at the company. When everyone had spoken, I said, "I guess I didn't speak clearly enough, for I asked you all to tell me who you are, not what you do." I then gave them an example: "I have a beautiful, talented, supportive wife, a son of whom I am very proud because of who he is; I love the woods of New Hampshire, Pachelbel's "Canon in D major" played on a cello; I'm a tad competitive; I am a fan of the New England Patriots. This should tell you a little about who I am. *Now*, what I do is to speak to management teams, teach them how to listen, and get paid by them for doing this." I smiled. "Now let's try again. We'll go around the table, and tell me aspects of who you are without telling me what you do." Initially, the silence was deafening. Years ago a popular phrase among the "flower children" was "identity crises." Scores of people were having this self-diagnosis of confusion. The solution and prescribed treatment I gave to such people was basic. I would suggest that they write down what they valued. In that process they would discover who they were and who they were becoming. It's what you bring to the job that defines you, not the job itself. Who one is always trumps whatever it is that one *does*. I owe so much to others who have contributed to the miles I have traveled. You and your mother are at the top of the list. In a significant relationship one finds out more about oneself than about the other person. This discovery ranges from priorities that matter, such as values clarified, and areas where growth can take place. The person who grows the most covers more territory where it counts, which is the area within each of us. I thank the Good Lord that He has shown me a great deal about myself and causes me to realize there still is room for growth.

Love, Always, Dad

No Whining
February 19, 2015

Son,

Classic Philosophers, Clinical Psychologists and Orthodox Theologians all agree that we live in a world that relentlessly challenges people wherever and whenever they have or will live. Life always will be a test. The stations of our mind, to wit, our perceptions will determine if we will live in a world of reality. President Theodore Roosevelt has been quoted as saying, "Complaining about a problem without posing a solution is called whining." Those with solutions are rarely those filled with fear or negativity in their disposition. There is an African proverb that goes *when the root is deep there is no reason to fear the wind.* Too often too many people spend time investing in shallow thought and frivolous activity. I thank the Good Lord that when I look at your life there is nothing shallow about you or your thoughts or activity. This Lenten season offers an opportunity for all people to reflect daily on their depth of "rootedness" past, present and future. The good news is that there is a "Water of Life" that covers all of these dimensions. What is wonderfully refreshing for me to know is of your commitment to drink deeply and daily of this Water, and thus no "whining" from you.

Love, Always, Dad

Leadership and Learning
March 5, 2015

Son,

After your mom was shot, I resigned from the positions I held in Miami and we moved to New Hampshire. Needing an income, I started a little business which was named CODE. It was an acronym which stood for the "Challenge Of Developing Excellence." It could be applied to just about anything, ranging from relationships, business, teaching, speaking, whatever. The reason this came to be was due to the conviction of two obvious principles. One, if you are doing anything, do it excellently. Secondly, learning is a life-long adventure and the pursuit of knowledge and wisdom are the critical parts. It's interesting that the word 'disciple' in the Greek language is *mathetes*, which literally means a "learner." Anyone who stops learning is old, whether they are twenty or eighty. *We don't grow old; we become old by not growing. Leadership and learning are essential to each other.* Reading about our country's military conflicts, it's obvious that there always will be risks and costs to actions taken. But they are far less than the long range risks of comfortable inaction. Thus I have not only pride in what you do but, more significantly, for who you are choosing to become day by day.

Love, Always, Dad

Heart of Champions
April 14, 2015

Son,

While in college, our basketball team played other schools in the Boston Garden. It was a phenomenal experience for someone like me who was an avid Boston Celtic fan. Bob Cousy, Bill Sharmon, Tom Heinsohn, Bill Russell, and Jim Loscutoff were winning all sorts of championships. After our preliminary game was over, our team sat right behind the Celtic Bench! Wow, what an experience! Bill Russell was on the team when they won eleven NBA Championships. He said this: "The heart of champions has to do with the depth of your motivation and how well your mind and body react to pressure - that is being able to do what you do best under maximum pain and stress." (Russell & Branch, 1979) When there are no challenges anybody can act calm, cool and collected. Challenges may come physically, mentally and spiritually, for life is all three. True Champions are found in this everyday life as well as on the athletic fields. The reason? As it is written, "God has not given us the spirit of fear or timidity but a spirit of power, love and self-control."[85] Champions embrace this reality in the face of anything. It's why you are the leader you are.

Love and Admiration, Always, Dad

---

85   2 Timothy 1:7

Using Time, Talents, Opportunities
April 17, 2015

Son,

When in high school, I worked summers for an Italian stonemason. It was an incredible learning and loving experience: learning because Leo was artistic, patient and proud of his work; loving, because when he found out that I had no normal home situation, he had his wife send a sandwich every day for his young helper. To this day I blame my hairline on the hot peppers she put in every sandwich, including even peanut butter! What I loved about Leo's work was the fact that when it was finished, there it stood—visible, strong and enduring! So I thought I would proudly follow his example. Then my path took some turns: I became a College Baseball Coach, Presbyterian Minister, Senior V.P. of Human Resources, then Reality Therapist! However, the constant with all of these pursuits was people. I thought that stone walls were durable in high school, but since then I learned of something else that was lasting. I learned that whatever you do in the way of developing mind, talent and character, one can be assured that their achievements are for eternity. Daniel Webster put it beautifully when he wrote:

If we work upon marble, it will perish;
If we work upon brass, time will efface it;
If we rear temples, they will crumble into dust.
But if we work upon immortal minds,
If we imbue them with high principles,

With the just fear of God and of their fellow men;
We engrave upon these tablets something
which no time can efface,
But which will brighten to all eternity.
(Burrowes, n.d.)

The key *is to use what we have of time, talent, brains and opportunity.*
Whatever evolution takes place when these are fully used, the
constant is the development of your talents for the benefit of
others. Knowing the final outcome is not as important as having
a goal of making a positive difference day by day and knowing,
when it's over, that you gave it your best shot, whatever it is you
have done. Just don't put hot peppers on peanut butter sandwiches!

Love, Always, Dad

Co-Laboring with God
May 11, 2015

Son,

One of my all-time favorite quotes is by Oliver Cromwell who said, "Put your trust in God, and keep your powder dry." (Simpson & Speake, 2008) I don't know if he had ever read Plato but he might have, for Plato said; "We are twice armed if we fight with faith." (Hagopian Institute, 2008) The best leaders in any pursuits are those who realize that life, to be at its best, is a co-laboring experience. The great reality which transcends imagination is that, if we so choose, our co-laborer is God. It is this awareness which enables any of us not only to have a special day today, but a great fulfilling future as well.

Love, Always, Dad

Attractor Fields
October 17, 2015

Son,

One of the things I have observed from the perspective of being a "shrink" is that many people, mostly men, have a 'functional identity'—to wit, their sense of self is tied to what they do rather than who they are and who they are becoming. Understandable but, in reality, dehumanizing. If a person has talent and a good work ethic, he or she can probably do a multitude of things, find fulfillment and satisfaction and discover once again that it is who they are and who they become that is the key to fulfillment. The circumstances may vary, the responsibilities evolve but in the final analysis it boils down to what is on the inside that matters most. Meister Eckhart was a 14th century Christian mystic and poignantly gave the following insight:

> *The outer work can never be small if the inner one is great. Neither can the outer work can be great or good where the inner work is weak or nil.*

(Eckhart, 1924)

As has been noted by many, that which uplifts life is the working together of heart and mind. This is the core truth of the world's great spiritual traditions. Dr. Hawkins, who wrote the classic *Power vs. Force*, said it cogently: "We change the world not by what we say or do but as a consequence of what we have become." (Clark, n.d.) Science has an understanding of energy patterns called attractor fields. The name *attractor* is given to an identifiable pattern that emerges from a mass. Without making this TFT a 2,000 page tome, let us come to the point. When a person such as yourself embraces the reality of what Paul wrote to Timothy—"God has not given us the spirit of timidity, but of power, love and a sound mind"[86]—you become an "attractor field." The God-given energy has a positive impact regardless of the vocational pattern in your life. This is another way of saying that I take pride and admiration for who you are and the impact you have on others, over and above the particulars of what you do. Although I do admit that what you do is very, very impressive.

Love, Always, Dad

---

86   2 Timothy 1:7

Awesome Awareness
November 3, 2015

Son,

O ne of the most puzzling lines that I ever heard being sung was not from Frank Sinatra or Elvis Presley or any other popular vocalist. It was taken from a hymn and the line is, "Take Time to Be Holy." (Longstaff, ca. 1882) When I first heard this I said to myself, "Eternity wouldn't be enough time for me to be holy"! Secondly, I thought I was in deep doodoo, especially given the fact that my time to get better at things I deemed important, such as Athletics, Studies and Women, was already utilizing all the time that I had. I thought "holiness" was something for Mother Theresa or the Benedictine or Jesuit Priesthood. What I didn't understand was that this "taking time to be holy" principle was not more minutes or hours *as much as it was an awesome awareness*! This was incredibly awakening because rather than excluding Athletics, Studies and Women, or any Professional Pursuits or Social Interactions, *it was including all of these and more*. Holiness involves a particular kind of engagement with people, with the world and with all that is. It is an engagement that includes love, joy and peace. These three qualities are the manifestations of having taken and incessantly continuing to take time to be holy. *It's all the time*; throughout all the day and *whatever* it is that we are doing with all of God's creatures and all of God's Creation, including even women! The thing I discovered in my journey is that true Holiness is being fully human, fully alive. This is the result of a double 'A,' to wit, Awesome Awareness of God's continual Presence. Enjoy this day, my Captain.

Love, Always, Dad

Distinct Destiny
November 15, 2015

Son,

When I wrote the TFT below in January of 2007, your career as a pilot was just beginning. Now you have been rated as a Certified Instructor in two distinctly different planes: a C-17 and a C-21; a Chief Eval Officer; Chief Safety Officer in Kuwait and at Scott Air Force Base; Pilot of the Year; a Flight Commander and an Aircraft Commander; serving as a member of the General Staff. Holy Mackerel! You know the one designation which means the most to me? It is, *Son*. Regardless of what lies before you in this crazy world in which we live, whatever titles, awards, achievements and titles you earn or are bestowed upon you; whatever or however long you remain in the Air Force, again, *Son* is the one I cherish. Why? Because of the man you have become. This latest challenge you met with your flight by listening and leading, is just another example. Congratulations!

Love, Always, Dad

Son,

I always was sure you were born for a distinct purpose. I was so convinced of this that I spoke of it at your Dedication Service as an infant in a Service at the First Presbyterian Church of St. Louis. This awareness on my part has never for one day left my consciousness. When through the years you would receive awards at the various schools you attended, I was never surprised; when you were singled out at Cardigan, or the Brooks Prep school as being "noble minded," I was not surprised; and when at the Air Force Academy, Major Nicholson said you were the finest cadet that he had ever had, likewise I was not surprised. (You may recall what I said to him in response. :) You have that "intangible" quality which cannot be analyzed with measuring devices of any kind. It is a quality of the Spirit. It is a passionate controlled strength that is manifested in humility, indefatigable work ethic and consistency. A man of prayer, who yet at the right time can use language that would make a Russian Cossack blush, I am confident that although the particulars of your career have not been revealed, that whatever they will be, will continue to bring glory to the God you love and a deep and abiding satisfaction in your heart of hearts. As you go forward one day at a time, rest assured of the constant company of our Lord, and my love and pride in watching you leave your mark simply by being the man you have become.

Love, Dad

Selective Thinking
November 19, 2015

Son,

There has been a lot of bad news lately, and if we don't seek out or recall good news, it could be awfully depressing. How we react to circumstances needs to be appropriate to the severity of the situation. However, *situations* come and go and we need to choose the *thoughts* which will dominate our spirit. This is the emphasis in all healthy spiritual belief systems. The important aspect is to rise above the kind of stuff which happened in Paris [terrorist massacre] and, unfortunately, continues to happen in too many places, too many times. Peterson put it as well as anyone I have read when he wrote, "As a single footstep will not make a path on the earth, so a single thought will not make a pathway in the mind. To make a deep physical path, we walk again and again. To make a deep mental path, we must think over and over the kind of thoughts we wish to dominate our lives." (Peterson, 1972) *This is the principle of selective thinking, not a denial of the existence of pain or evil.* We deal with both of these by displacement. We open the front door of our minds to good guests (thoughts) and let these, by their presence, push out the uninvited. The key is keeping the front door open to good guys (thoughts). We profit from positive reality by constant reinforcement. The results are healthy, life supporting and transformative, not just for the person who makes this commitment but for all those with whom he or she interacts. It's probably just one of the reasons people really enjoy your company.

Love, Always, Dad

Focus
February 23, 2016

Son,

One of the basics in life is that whatever a person focuses upon becomes magnified. Unfortunately, there are those who focus on their screw-ups of yesterday or yesteryear. Many people are their own worst critics because they focus on the delusional thinking called "perfection." "What is reality?" they ask. It's turning not only *horse-shit but our own shit into fertilizer! The key is always being a first-rate version of yourself rather than a second-rate version of someone else.* Our circumstances will always change and, while this is reality, the one constant for being stable is that our inner core stays solid, or what is referred to as "being centered." Lao Tzu is said to have written, "There is no need to run outside for better seeing... Rather, abide at the center of your being. For the more you leave it, the less you learn. Search your heart and see. The way to do is to be." And as the Good Book says, "Christ in you, the hope of glory."[87] Our humanity awakens us to areas that we need to work on. How great is this? It's spectacular, because we can embrace fully the reality that the best is yet to come! It's not so much *what* we do but rather *how* we do it, *becoming all we can be in the process.*

Love, Always, Dad

---

87   Colossians 1:27b

Who Can You Trust?
April 10, 2016

Son,

When I was seventeen and had graduated from high school, I received a full scholarship to Milford Prep as a PG (postgraduate). The purpose of my going back to school was to get my grades up, develop physically and get a year's coaching under Jerry Pepper, one of the original "Blocks of Granite!"[88] I was quite excited, and the school invited scholarship recipients to a dinner before the season began. Living in Bridgeport, I needed to get some transportation, and I asked an adult I knew if he would allow me to use his car. At the time I was living with a milkman and his family. After the adult I asked said he would let me use his car, I made my way to his house and was waiting for him to come home from the office where he worked. Time went on and he didn't arrive. I called the watering hole [bar] where he hung out and asked if he was there. The fellow who answered held the receiver up, called him by name and said I was on the phone. The response was loud enough for me to hear: "Tell him I'm not here." I rode my bike back to the milkman's house, and he allowed me to take his stand-up milk truck to Milford. As I arrived, the dinner party had already ended, and the other folks had left or were in

---

88 "Blocks of Granite" was a nickname for the outstanding line-men of Fordham University's Football team during the early 1930s.

the process of leaving. I cried and cussed driving the truck back to Bridgeport. I had trusted the person who said he would meet me and that I could use his car. The most damaging pain to our heart and soul is being betrayed by a person we count on. While I can forgive a person for anything, it doesn't mean I'll ever trust him again. Later that year, however, I started to be exposed to the Scriptures and came across this text: "Trust in the Lord with all your heart, and do not rely on your own insight. In all your ways acknowledge Him and He will make straight your paths."[89] Not only does our Savior keep His Word, but he keeps us under His wings forever, wherever our journey takes us. I know this because He has kept me. By the way, the person who didn't show up with his car was the same person who had arranged for my kidnapping when I was eight months old. He was my biological father. I made a commitment to you that I would be to you the kind of father I never had.

Love, Always, Dad

---

89   Proverbs 3:5-6 RSV

Love Is Not Passive
April 18, 2016

Son,

A word about love. I once thought that a person could have love, like you have a car, or golf clubs, or a house. But then I realized that having anything is not the same as being anything. Love is not having; in reality, love is a productive activity of knowing, affirming, enjoying, caring and responding in a manner that is self-renewing and self-increasing. One can't *fall* in love, for that is a contradiction in itself. As Fromm insightfully noted, "one can only *stand* in love or *walk* in love... *for falling denotes passivity.*" (Fromm, 1976) As you and I know, there is nothing passive about love. Thank God! Sometimes people who are married tend to feel the other individual is theirs, as in a possession like a piece of property. The two no longer make an effort to be lovable and cease *loving* each other and evolve into ownership. Marriage is not the problem, but each person must make the choice of perpetually *being* a loving partner— *being* a loving parent, being a loving brother or sister, or son or daughter. Love is never static. Paul (the Apostle, not your dad) said it beautifully and cogently: "Love is patient and kind . . . not arrogant or rude . . . Love bears all things . . . Love never ends . . . As for knowledge, it will pass away for our knowledge is imperfect . . . Now we see in a mirror dimly, but then face to face. Now I know in part, but then I shall understand fully, even as I have been fully understood. So faith, hope and love abide, but the greatest of these is love."[90] It is why love will always be our aim and, by God's grace, our experience.

Love, Always, Dad

90 1 Corinthians 13:4-13 RSV

Birth versus Air Show
May 11, 2016

Son,

What a great few days to be in the presence of you, Amanda and Paul Liam![91] Having your son come out of what I have termed the "Love Oven" on Mother's Day was rather spectacular! Obviously, your life has been changed forever. The setting at the hospital, the staff and accommodations were all terrific. Watching the tender moments between all of those present is in my everlasting memory book. One of the things you talked about almost as an aside was the fact that all of this was happening just a few days before the great air show to be conducted this week on base. And that you were chosen to be the command pilot of the C-17 at the show. Before we left, you mentioned casually that you were not going to be in the pilot's seat you had been chosen for, because you have had such little sleep during this advent of the next "Mac." This was a candid testimony to your wisdom in stepping aside from what many coveted and would be hesitant to assign to another. You not only have shown tremendous love and gratitude for your son being born but also demonstrated your sense of duty and excellence of service standard, knowing your lack of sleep these past few days could potentially negatively impact the air show. You mentioned this rather quite casually, *but* it did not

---

91 Mac's first child was born three days earlier.

slip past Grandpa Grizz. Your "duty, honor and country" lifestyle is without doubt a treasure I will always cherish, regardless of the particulars of your professional career and whatever this may entail in future days. It's not the particulars of what you do that matters most; it's the quality you bring to whatever it is that you do. Man, husband, father, son, pilot, ADO,[92] *regardless of the specifics—it's you that matters most, and it always will be that way.* Thank you for enriching my life by virtue of your being.

Love, Always, Dad

---

92   Assistant Director of Operations—3rd in command of operations at his Air Force base.

Embrace of Love
May 12, 2016

Son,

With the birth of your son, my thoughts have been dominated by the continual presence of the Lord of all creation. Recently, I was driving down one of the beautiful country roads and was overwhelmed by the beauty surrounding me: the great oaks, tall evergreens, clear lakes and ponds, all incredibly beautiful! I felt as if God was embracing me in the arms of His creation as a symbol of His arms around and protecting and reassuring me of His love. The peace that overcame me was beyond words. It reminded me of the Psalm where David wrote, "Where shall I go from Thy Spirit? Or whither shall I flee Thy Presence? If I ascend to the heavens, Thou art there! If I make my bed in Sheol, Thou art there! If I take the wings of the morning and dwell in the uttermost parts of the sea, even there Thy hand shall lead me, and Thy right hand shall hold me. For thou didst form my inward parts, thou didst knit me together in my mother's womb. I praise Thee for Thou art wonderful."[93] The reality of what David wrote is mine, and yours, and your son's as well! As you know, I did not have the arms of a loving mother or father growing up, but God saw that His love would one day overwhelm me. All that I know, any degrees that I have or experiences of

---

93   Psalm 139:7-10, 13-14 RSV

satisfaction do not come close to what and how our Savior has blessed me with by His Presence, wherever I am and whatever it is that I am doing. You are blessed with a loving wife and mother for your son. The combination of her arms and yours, along with our Lord's continual Presence wherever you go and whatever the particulars of what you do, bodes incredibly well for a future that, because of Him, knows no limits. This, my son, is just the beginning, for the best is yet to come.

Love, Always, Dad

Words Do Matter

August 7, 2016

Son,

In my life and practice, what I have observed about words is the depth or the shallowness with which they are used. Anybody can say just about anything, yet the power of what they are saying is in large part *dependent on the depth of character of the speaker.* The words may be simple, like "If you need me, I'll be there for you." They mean nothing unless the person uttering the words has demonstrated a track record you can count on. *Then, and only then, do the words mean something.* I have a goal to never say something seriously that I don't mean. When your mother was shot, our lives were changed forever. From that moment on, it was apparent that how we lived, where we lived, what and where I would do my work would change. Not knowing the future, I knew certainly we would not be living in Miami. I looked into the mirror and repeated to myself the pledge I had made to her, which was "Regardless of circumstances, for better or for worse, I will be there for you." The horrific shooting provided the opportunity for me to choose to embrace the reality that *words do matter.* As a result, you are here, with your partner for life and now, in addition, your son, all of which are our immeasurable treasures. Speaking of the importance of words, do you think that it's a coincidence that the Gospel of John begins in this manner: "In the beginning was the Word, and the Word was with God, and the Word was God . . . In Him was life and the life was the light of men. The Light shines in darkness, and the darkness has not overcome it."[94] Words do mean a great deal and I admire immensely how you use them and the person you are, who stands behind them.

Love, Always, Dad

---

94   John 1:1, 4-5 RSV

Indy 500 Life Maintenance

August 30, 2016

Son,

The Indy 500 car race was this past weekend, and fans who weren't there were glued to the TV! Talented drivers are critical, *but* maintenance and refueling are as critical to victory as the racing itself. Why? Because the higher the demand, the more frequent the need for renewal! Many people are more concerned about maintenance of things than they are about taking care of themselves! Just as vehicles and planes have key parts, so do we and none should be neglected if we are to perform at our best, à la a C-17—or a human who is fully alive!

Love, Always, Dad

The Best Is Yet To Come

October 5, 2016

Son,

When you change the way you look at things, the things you look at change. Furthermore all change is a teacher. It's one of the reasons a person can realistically embrace the truism that "the best is yet to come". There was a saying I heard years ago that went like this: "I don't know what the future holds, but I do know who holds the future." *When an individual has a "centering" aspect to their life, they can not only handle life "somehow", but handle it joyfully, triumphantly and consistently. The reason is plain: peace, fulfillment and joy cannot be purchased; they are the result of living every day with love, gratitude and grace.* It's a key that you've embraced in your journey, both personally and professionally, and it shows.

Love, Always and Forever, Dad

Awe and Reverence
October 8, 2016

Son,

Some of our Jewish friends are currently observing what they refer to as the "Ten Days of Awe." These days begin with Rosh Hashanah and end with Yom Kippur. Awe is something that happens when the mind is clear and the heart is at rest. Choosing the focus of one's mind is essential. Will I think daily of the idiot that shot your mother? Will I think of a father who had his son kidnapped because he was divorcing his wife and did not want her to have custody of the child? Will I think of people who are whack jobs? Will I think of simple mistakes like the garage door being left open and the dog going off on an exploratory jaunt to places she had never been? If so, at the end of the day I will not be in awe. However, what if I choose to heed Sarah Ban Breathnach's advice when she said, "Gratitude bestows reverence, allowing us to encounter transcendent moments of awe that change forever how we experience life and the world"? (Breathnach, 1996) The choice as to how we look at things and interpret them makes the difference, enabling us to see each day with awe and sleep well and walk upright with peace within.

Love, Always and Forever, Dad

Spiritual DNA
October 12, 2016

Son,

We all have DNA. As you know, this is the abbreviation that stands for deoxyribonucleic acid. It's the substance that carries genetic information. I've noticed over the years that some lawyers, some men and women of science, and some misfits blame behavior and irrational acts on one's DNA. So people like Viktor Frankl, Rollo May, Winston Churchill, Curtis Le May, and Eddie Rickenbacker became who they became because of their DNA? This is classic psychological and scientific manure. *People become who they become because of a commitment to* Nothingness *or, by contrast, a commitment to excellence motivated by purpose.* We all have this potential because our fundamental DNA is our spirituality, and this implies accountability. It's basic and it's obvious in your life and will be in your son's life because of your modeling and God's Grace.

Love, Always and Forever, Dad

Follow Your Bliss

November 3, 2016

Son,

Any person, be they man or woman, in following their "bliss" are freed from societal pressures. People with this vision are empowered to live a life that is impactful. Why? The answer is rather basic; it is the fulfillment of that which is potential in each of us. This is not an ego trip; it is rather an adventure to bring to fulfillment a gift that only each person can give to the world, which is him or herself. In a very real sense, this is what the teachings of the great traditions have always been about, be it Judaism or Christianity or Buddhism. The reason this is not plain at times is that religious leaders, be they clergy or others, reduce these great teachings and traditions to a series of rules and regulations. In ignoring the mythical impact of a Job, or a Daniel, or a David and Goliath, they fail to see what God can and wishes to do in all human instruments. Being the complete self you are designed to be takes constant reflection which produces continual renewal, regardless of circumstances, because of the reality of the Sacred in all of that which is alive. This is not a drag or a burden because in so doing, one is "electrified or energized" with the passion of freedom for being all one is. True bliss is available to all, whether they are artists, writers, leaders in industry, medicine or military, finance or frontiers of space. Bliss is embracing what the sages throughout time have recognized as a spiritually inspired life, regardless of the particulars! It is why I am sure you will follow your bliss.[95]

Love, Always and Forever, Dad

Photographed by: Thomas G. Wilson

---

95   Mac was wrestling with a career choice between two mutually exclusive but wonderful options. The author was encouraging him to "follow his bliss."

Career Choices
November 27, 2016

Son,

O ne of the realities of life is that options are usually presented to those who work their asses off and live within the context of timeless values. This sentence epitomizes you and where you are in your professional career and personal life. You have always made thoughtful decisions based on your commitment to excellence regarding faith, family and professional focus. Your gifts are obvious, and your commitment to ever-increasing excellence, across the board, is the reason you are in this current situation of various professional organizations pursuing you hot and heavy. *Take a deep breath, let go, and let the Lord calm you with the inner assurance that He will enable you to sense the direction you shall take with accompanying inner peace.* Your being true to the things you believe in has always been obvious to me, and this is one of the reasons, whatever the particular choice you make, I am with you one hundred percent plus, now and forever!

Love, Always and Forever, Dad

Pearl Harbor Anniversary and Return to U.S. Air Force Academy

December 7, 2016

Son,

Seventy-five years ago today the Japanese attacked Pearl Harbor—it was, President Roosevelt said, "a date of infamy." Yet another day, an attack was launched on September 11, 2001, and more people were killed, the majority of whom—unlike those slain on December 7, 1941—were not in the military. The focus I choose to have is on the brave men and women and how they responded to these two awful, painful days. Heroism and sacrifice became a way of life. I don't need to remind you that the day after September 11, you applied to the Air Force Academy, and your life, and your family's life, was changed forever. As your dad, what do I choose to focus upon? The evil bastards who planned and committed these acts? The pain and suffering that followed, the scars that will remain? No—not any of these are my focus or habitual thoughts. My focus is on themes like bravery, sacrifice, commitment, heroism and preparation for days ahead, and ways of living in a world where the reality of good and evil exists. My professional responsibility is to stress the importance of teaching people to choose a perpetual optimism, regardless of pain or loss. Why? The answer is clear, from both a clinical perspective and personal experience. *Optimism is a force multiplier. The energy released from optimism to face challenging days ahead is immeasurable.* The key is an optimism grounded in the reality of clear thinking, hard work, a cause beyond one's ego and a centering within one's self that transcends circumstances, whatever they may be! I could choose to focus on the fact that my biological father hired someone to have me kidnapped at age eight months, which resulted in my growing up in the inner city without any parents; or choose to focus on God's grace and "Eskimos"[96] that came out of nowhere. I could focus on the evil of September 11th or the heroic, selfless decision of service you made to attend the United States Air Force Academy because of that attack— not to mention the fact that now you will return to the Academy in the capacity of a AOC![97] *There is no denying the fact that people perceive the world through whatever paradigm they live in.* You and I share a paradigm based on a shared set of assumptions, to wit, "We can handle all things through Christ." This paradigm was proclaimed and embodied by those who, 2000 years ago, made a commitment to the Christ of Christmas, and to this day it has been demonstrated rather dramatically by you and your fellow service men and women.

Love, Always and Forever, Dad

---

96 'Eskimos' refers to a story the author tells often, admitting that he has had a lot of Eskimos in his life: Two men were in a bar discussing whether or not God existed. One man said he was an atheist but he had almost believed in God one time when he was stranded in a vehicle in Alaska during a severe storm and he ran out of gas. He promised God that if he got out of there, he would believe in God. The other man said, "Well, here you are. How come you still don't believe in God?" The atheist said, "Oh, God had nothing to do with it. An Eskimo came along."

97 Air Officer Commanding. Ever since graduating from the Air Force Academy in 2006, Mac's long-term goal was to return to the Academy under this capacity, to be the officer responsible for military training, and character and leadership development for one of the forty squadrons of cadets as their leader, advisor and mentor.

Thanksgiving for John Glenn
December 9, 2016

Son,

One of the great messages of this Christmas season is received through a multiple assortment of classic Christmas hymns and carols. I love them, for most are sung with joy and carry the message articulated by Christ Himself. One of my favorites is "Hark the Herald Angels Sing." One of the verses has in it the words, "Born that man no more may die." (Wesley, Whitefield, & Mendelssohn, 1739) Some ask, "Where did this crazy idea come from?" The answer is clear—it came from the greatest teacher who ever lived, who said during His ministry, "He that lives and believes in Me will never die."[98] "But, But, But," come the cries of thousands, "My parents died; my friends have died." However, a person's uniqueness of personhood is not their body, thank God! A person's essence is what is *contained in* their body. John Glenn's spirit separated from his body yesterday, but while he used the combination of his body and spirit to serve his country—and we all benefited from his role, which ranged from his service in the Second World War to the Korean War, as one of the original seven astronauts, and in the U.S. Senate, etc.—it was not his body but his spirit that made the difference and that will never die! One of the many insightful statements he made was "The most

---

98   John 11:26

important thing we can do is to inspire young minds." (Astronaut-Senator 2016) Even though his body is no longer here on earth, his spirit lives forever, and his inspiration will as well. One of the primary aspects and purposes of Christ's birth was to remove the myopic fable of humanism that life is bound and tied to physical years, and then our influence is over. Not really! The things we do that are important transcend our physical years, just as our spirit does. I hope that people everywhere will find *the gift of this realization* under the tree this year. So last night I added to my thanksgiving list what John Glenn embodied with his time on earth, and what he will continue to do from his perspective and the place he now occupies with his eternal spirit, which will continue to be the essence of his being.

Love, Always and Forever, Dad

Icebox

December 29, 2016

Son,

Observing your son, an eight-month bundle of joy and responsibility, as he attempted to crawl on the floor, I was reflecting about the awesome changes that lie in store for him as well as for you and his mother! But change is a reality of life and therefore something to be welcomed with confidence and enthusiasm. Here's a crazy example of this inevitable truism. As a child, I lived in many places with many different people, but one thing that was common to all of them was something called an "icebox"—not a refrigerator, or freezer, but an icebox! Under the icebox was a large metal container for water from the melting ice. The ice man would come by on a regular routine with his horse drawn wagon, yelling, "Ice or rags!" He was delivering ice and also collecting rags that people wanted to throw away. If as a child you were misbehaving, the threat was that you'd be given to the "rag man"! Upon reflection, I notice that the main emphasis or awareness on the part of many people is observing the enormous circumstantial changes in the outer world—like our having no more iceboxes. In countless other areas we obviously have made great strides and positive changes; but in spite of all these, far too many people are woefully unaware of the essentials of a total person—whether we are being fully human, fully alive. Without a rich understanding of our inner needs over against our wants, of goals that are transitory over against those that are eternal, our collective future as a society will be living morally, spiritually and psychologically in an era of the "icebox." I thank the Good Lord that your priorities are based on those values which are timeless and that your inner-stabilizer will never melt nor ever be outdated!

Love, Always and Forever, Dad

Chance and Choice

February 6, 2017

Son,

M any, many years ago when I was a senior in high school,[99] a complete stranger approached me at the end of football practice. He introduced himself and asked if I would be interested in going to a prep school as a postgrad and playing for Gerry Pepper, who was not only the head football coach but the headmaster of the school as well. The stranger also mentioned that tuition would not be an issue! Living without parents, I didn't have anyone to ask, and simply said yes. In retrospect, evaluated my life and the lives of numberless others, *I've observed that chance and choice converge to make us who we are.* You've done exceedingly well with these two realities.

Love, Always and Forever, Dad

---

99   An underfunded inner city school in Bridgeport, Connecticut.

Dealing with Adversity
February 11, 2017

Son,

Benjamin Franklin wrote, "The things which hurt, instruct." (Brooks, 1898) Perhaps that is why it's said that life's most painful lessons, even when self-inflicted, are also the most valuable. Yet reality is such that pain teaches us something only if we are willing to learn from it. What I have learned personally and professionally is that real success in life is largely determined by how well we deal with adversity. Growing up without parents in the inner city, I learned some incredible lessons, albeit some rather painfully. One basic lesson is that life is not always fair. Our real success in life will be determined by how we deal with it. We can run from it or face it; we can surrender or quit. I understand why some people quit, and I will never judge them pejoratively. Fortunately, by Grace I learned about Jesus Christ and His promise to be with me always. When I am attentive and consciously aware of this reality, I can awaken each day with hope and go to bed at night with a peace that comes from Him, and not circumstances. It is this reality that enables a person, any person, to be "more than a conqueror."[100] You have learned this and it will serve you well.

Love, Always and Forever, Dad

---

100   Romans 8:37

John Wooden on Intentness

February 14, 2017

Son,

O ne of the most interesting dinner conversations I ever had was at the Basketball Hall of Fame in Springfield, Massachusetts. I was seated with the legendary basketball coach John Wooden. It was an evening of listening and learning. Many things were worth sharing, but one that stood out was his emphasis on intentness—the ability, in his words, to stay on course, not so much in *wanting* something as it is in *doing* something. His message was clear—real achievement takes time: "Be persistent. Be determined. Be tenacious. Be completely determined to reach your goal. That's intentness. If you stay intent and your ability warrants it, you will eventually reach the top of the mountain." (Salzgeber, 2017) In retrospect, that evening with him probably contributed to these nineteen years of TFTs.

Love, Always and Forever, Dad

(P.S. Wooden's autographed picture hangs just outside our library.)

Schweitzer on Success
February 18, 2017

Son,

Perhaps the most multitalented individual I have ever studied was Albert Schweitzer—a notable theologian, philosopher, social thinker and medical doctor, not to mention that at one time he was considered the greatest interpreter of Bach and eminent performer of Bach's music on the organ! He authored several books, and in one of them declared, "Civilization is then twofold in its nature: it realizes itself the supremacy of reason, first over the forces of nature, and secondly over the dispositions of men." (Schweitzer, 1947) Not a bad premise, given the injunction of Jesus to His followers to think clearly. Schweitzer's advice was simple when it came to being successful: "Success is not the key to happiness. Happiness is the key to success. If you love what you are doing, you will be successful."

Love, Always and Forever, Dad

Success Peace of Mind

March 11, 2017

Son,

One of the keys to learning is asking questions, and humans do this intuitively in childhood. Unfortunately, there are teachers and parents who don't encourage this trait for many reasons. My guess is that some teachers and parents are embarrassed by not knowing how to answer. Coach John Wooden was asked "What is your definition of success?" His reply was "Success is peace of mind, which is a direct result of self-satisfaction in knowing you have made the effort to be the best of which you are capable. Never try to be better than someone else; never cease trying to be the best you can be—one is under your control; the other isn't." (Wooden & Jamison, 2007) I remember saying to a youngster, "I don't care whether you get As, Bs or Cs—I just want you to be able to look into the mirror and be able to say, 'I did my best.'" Obviously, you listened!

Love, Always and Forever, Dad

School of Life
May 4, 2017

Son,

Someone asked me, "Of all the schools you've attended, including undergrad, grad, post grad, etc. etc., from which school did you learn the most and which school prepared you the most?" The answer was one he didn't expect, for the school which prepared me the most is the one in which I'm still enrolled; it's the school of life. Without a doubt, it's the most challenging, the most demanding and the most rewarding. Life is least challenging or easiest when one at some level resists learning, or mentally withdraws from reality. To "climb the mountain" of knowledge, of love, of wisdom is, without doubt, the most challenging. Seeing that the focus of my career as a coach, minister, shrink, therapist, etc., etc., all involve working with people, *the obvious learning experience was and is that I cannot see inside anyone.* Others through their writings or personal testimony of life must reveal themselves. *The only person I can study from the inside is myself.* In retrospect, I see that the periods in life which were the hardest, or the most painful, were the periods in which I grew the most. One of the great values in attempting to be a jock was learning not to grumble when pushed further and farther on all levels but to adjust, as the Pats did in the last Super Bowl.[101] The school of life takes no semesters off, and has no so-called safe places, as some current academic environs provide. The great news about this school of life is that learning and preparing to have a significant impact is never ending. I delight, as your dad and a biased observer, that you are fully enrolled in this greatest school offered to thinking, goal-oriented human beings.

Love Always, Now and Forever, Dad

---

101 The New England Patriots were behind 3-28 points in the third quarter of the Super Bowl but came back to win the game 34-28 in overtime.

No Quick Fix
June 6, 2017

Son,

We live in the era of the "quick fix." Unfortunately, while this may be possible for a flat tire or burned-out light bulb, it's not true for something serious. The problem, however, is that the quick fix is often applied to a person's health, be it physical or psychological. Pills and more pills seems to be the M.O. for treating people and the result is dependency, addiction or whatever! While meds are sometimes effective (for certain cases like bipolar or schizophrenic disorders), most often the pill approach is a shortcut for control rather than a remedy for recovery. The good news is that in the vast majority of cases, a remedy for renewal and recovery is possible. *The price is a radical commitment to a change of habits through the renewal of the mind.* With the right coaching, the process can be made clear. The evolution of the soul is a lifetime process, and substantive healing creates a total uplift of attitude and an enhanced spiritual awareness. The future then comes into existence, and the antique chains of the psyche are broken. You will be interested in seeing how this truth is presented or prostituted when working on your MA in Psyche of Leadership at Colorado State. Keep me posted.

Love, Always, Now and Forever, Dad

Father's Day
June 18, 2017

Son,

Ilt's fascinating to me that our Lord taught us to look at God as a "father image." When I first heard this, I wondered how to do it, inasmuch as my earthly father actually hired people to kidnap me at eight months of age. But the Lord went on to demonstrate by His own life that God our Father is approachable, affectionate, affirming, almighty and assuring! He clarified this to the disciples by saying, "Whoever has seen Me has seen the Father."[102] On this Father's Day, what can we know for certain about our Father God? Jesus went on to say, "I am the Way, the Truth and the Life, and no man comes to the Father but by Me"[103] and "I am with you always."[104] *Mac, the kind of father you are will convey to your son both responsibility and accountability in the context of constant love and encouragement.* This is what our Lord did and continues to do with us. He is your Lord, Savior and indwelling Presence as you continue on your journey of fatherhood. What a joy for me as your dad to behold. Happy Father's Day!

Love Always, Now and Forever, Dad

---

102   John 14:9
103   John 14:6
104   Matthew 28:20

Leadership

July 22, 2017

Son,

I am amazed that you and other officers are taking a course on leadership and psyche, but not surprised. Maslow summed up leadership pretty well when he said, "One can choose to go back toward safety or forward toward growth. Growth must be chosen again and again..." (Rose, 2016) *True leaders become great not because of their power but because of their ability to empower others.* The goal and gift of leadership is to produce more leaders, not more followers. What was so amazing about the Lord was that He empowered "ordinary" people to go out and change the world. And for Christ's sake, they did and are still doing it to this day! His leadership style was incredibly earth changing, and He told the learners who followed Him to go and do likewise.

Love Always, Now and Forever, Dad

Losing "Drama"
July 26, 2017

Son,

As I write this TFT, many, many, feelings well up within me. I looked at and admired your "Drama"[105] for decades! Her humor, her competitiveness, her laughter, enthusiasm and consistency made all those mother-in-law jokes ridiculous and as antiquated as the Philistine Age! You, my son, are rich indeed with priceless memories of her and being with her *which you have stored away in the vault of your heart.* You can carry that vault with you wherever you go and open it up at any time of day or night. It will never be stolen or taken away from you. The more you handle those memories, the brighter they will become, like polished stone. Now she has joined the line of many witnesses who have preceded her. There is a difference, though, for she will be yelling harder than all the rest rooting you on! I have great admiration for her and always will—and so will many, many others who remain on this side of Glory. Those who preceded her have now welcomed her with singing to eternal bliss and rest.

Love Always, Now and Forever, Dad

---

105   Mac called his maternal grandmother "Drama." She was his first and primary babysitter for the first six years after he was born, and they had a special relationship. At her memorial service, the author compared her to the greatest cheerleader of all time—always positive, always supportive, regardless of circumstances.

Drama and Love Eternal
July 27, 2017

Son,

Sometimes it takes an event to make sense out of great readings. The Scriptures are filled with a multitude of examples, but one stands out because of what our family experienced this week. The Apostle Paul waxed eloquently in his writings about gifts, and he pointed to three of them: Faith, Hope and Love. He said all three are great, and we know that all three can have a profound impact on everyone, from a bricklayer to an astronaut, from a scientist to a musician. But the one he singled out, one that stood above all the rest, is what epitomized your Drama—it was Love. She was a musician, a competitor, a social catalyst and a life enthusiast whose presence made a difference, but that which dominated was her love. The Apostle Paul went on to say that everything will pass away but Love, and that is why it is the greatest of the three. Just as love lasts forever, so will your Drama. It is why you never have to say goodbye to her.

Love, Always, Now and Forever, Dad

Think Clearly, Act Rationally, Live Purposefully

August 19, 2017

Son,

The problem of anxiety is that for many people, it never leaves. The source may differ, as well as the particulars. As a child, a person may have anxiety over the possibility of not having friends, or of making public mistakes, or of antagonizing others; then in adulthood, the anxiety may be over job loss or poor performance or missed opportunities. The way to overcome anxiety is by self-messaging rationally. Worrying about potential situations make them worse rather than improving them. One of the keys is for people to realize how senseless and self-defeating it is to keep worrying about this or that awful thing happening. *It appears that some people create their anxiety by focusing on the wrong thing.* When taking a class on public speaking, I noticed that some of those in the class were more worried about how the audience would respond rather than the depth and substantive facets of what they were saying. If a speaker has done his or her homework, it is not the speaker who must measure up, but the listeners. In life we are simply called upon to think clearly, act rationally and live purposefully. It appears that those who do suffer little anxiety. As the Good Book says, "Have no anxiety about anything, but in *everything* by prayer and supplication with thanksgiving, let your requests be made known to God and the peace of God will garrison your hearts and minds in Christ Jesus."[106]

Love Always, Now and Forever, Dad

---

106   Philippians 4:6-7

Teaching Cadets
August 28, 2017

Son,

I am very excited for you this morning for two reasons. The day after September 11th, you applied to the Air Force Academy because that unforgettable, heinous tragedy caused you to respond with a commitment to service for our country. Your life since that time has embodied that commitment. Your resolve to do everything you could to fortify our country has brought you challenges, required sacrifice and given you a sense of purpose far beyond the ordinary. Now this morning you will teach cadets at the very Academy that you graduated from, fulfilling one of the specific goals in your Air Force career: one day to return in order to inspire and motivate and challenge current cadets. There is a wonderful passage in Scriptures that comes to my mind: "Delight yourself in the Lord and He will give you the desires of your heart."[107] You have worked your ass off, volunteered for special missions, and have risen in rank and responded to demanding opportunities. Sometimes people seek the Lord's blessing as if it were a free lunch. But you have paid for this opportunity with your depth of service and preparation. I am fully confident that the cadets will sense that their teacher has worn the mantle of service. This combined with the Lord's faithfulness should embolden and

---

107   Psalm 37:4

empower you so that you walk into the class this morning with Him beside you. Your ethic and commitment was and is due to your call to serve God and country.

Love Always, Now and Forever, Dad

Eating Our Ice Cream Before It Melts
November 17, 2017

Son,

Reflection on the various circumstances we all face provides a wonderful opportunity for grading one's self. This reflection can be incredibly motivating as to how we are going to invest our time henceforth. Asking questions when awakened to how the clock keeps running is a fortuitous experience on many levels. For one, it places priorities in order as a result of clarifying our values. These values and priorities, of course, are critical to our personal identity. There are certain basic questions—like "Who am I? What is expected of me?" or, in particular, "What do I expect of myself?"— which will determine how we enjoy the days that are here and the days that are ahead. *These times of reflection are a wonderful opportunity for renewal that engenders inner peace and an optimism based on the reality of transience.* Put into words anyone can understand, we need to eat our ice cream before it melts. Every day is a gift, and to share this reality with those who matter most makes each day a celebration. Of course, the "ice cream" we choose is critical to our health, our longevity, our strength to be all we can be. Our minds enable our inner spirit to prioritize those subjects which matter most. This is why our goal to be fully human, fully alive is energized by our awareness that the clock is running. An awareness that each day matters is a freeing consciousness to live with an authenticity based on the eternal security of hearing, "Well done...enter now into the joy of your Master."[108]

Love Always, Now and Forever, Dad

---

108   Matthew 25:21

POST LOG

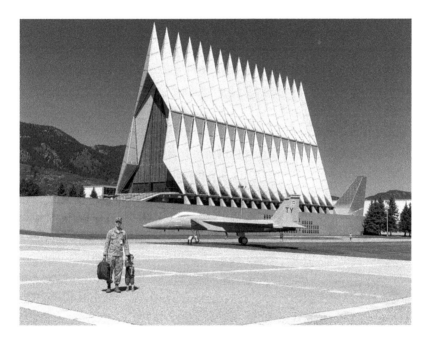

Mac and his son, Air Force Academy 2018

Remarks To Air Force Academy in Commemoration of 9/11

September 11, 2018

Good afternoon, my name is Major William MacVittie and I have the honor of leading and leaning alongside the Men and Women of Cadet Squadron 28. I'm also a proud member of the class of 2006. I joined the Air Force because of September 11th. I was a senior in high school in 2001, and at the time I thought I wanted to be a veterinarian, but that all changed on that Tuesday morning. I've flown C-17s and C-21s around the world. I've been to over 40 counties on 6 different continents. I've had the highest honor of taking men and women into combat, and the somber duty to bring home our fallen heroes. But for me that journey started sitting in Mr. Moody's math class. I had seen the images on CNN between periods, but word reached us right after the bell rang for calculus that the South Tower had fallen. I remember all of us just sitting there in silence. Too stunned to say anything. The only sound that broke the stillness was the soft crying of a girl in the next class over across the hall. She was weeping because that morning her dad was flying from Boston to LA, and at that moment she did not know if he was alive or dead. I remember the feeling of helplessness that permeated every aspect of that room. And the desire to do something. Eventually when Mr. Moody did speak, it was to remark that "things are going to change." And he was right. For me personally, I made my decision then and there that I wanted to do something to get back at those people. I started my application to the Air Force Academy the following day. So that's my why. All of you have your own reasons for being here. There is no "right answer" for why we choose to serve. But whatever your reason may be, I encourage you to hold on to it. Remind yourself of it every day. There will be hard times both here at The Academy and when you get out onto the front lines. Remember why you chose to be here in the first place, and that will propel you through the trials and tribulations that lay ahead. [109]

109   Mac was asked to address the entire US Air Force Academy community in their annual Remembrance Ceremony for September 11, 2001

Fini Flight
September 1, 2019

Son,

This special weekend[110] brings back memories that cannot be reduced to words. They are of your first Parents Weekend at the Academy in 2002. You had survived "Jack's Valley's" initiatory challenges and when you walked up to us, it appeared that you had grown taller than when you left for the Academy in June 2002! I want to say, with the passing of years, you have not shrunk at all! You embody the truism of the phrase *to stand tall*, unyielding, without retreating from the confrontation of danger or adversity, or unforeseen challenges. When a person Stands Tall in the classic sense, it is because his armor is made of eternal principles of honor, service and purpose beyond self. The world belongs to the man who can stand tall because he sees through pretensions and whose mind cannot be altered by the fear which springs from ignorance. He is great and able to stand tall, not because he can alter matter but because he can alter his state of mind. The day is always his who works with serenity and great aims, who embraces the One who said, "I am the light and whoever walks with me will never

---

110   This Parents' Weekend was Mac's final one as Air Officer Commanding for USAFA Squadron 28 for two academic years.

walk in darkness."[111] It is the epitome of standing tall. You have embraced this truth existentially; I salute you, and always will![112]

Love Always, Now and FOREVER, Dad

---

111 John 8:12
112 "Dollar Ride" and "Fini Flight" (see page 79) refer to the longstanding Air Force tradition of naming and celebrating a pilot's first and last flights in various aircraft.

During his tenure at the Air Force Academy, Mac
served as a pilot of the UV-18B *"Twin Otter" flying*
in support of the USAF Parachute Team known as
the Wings of Blue. Here his family celebrates his "fini
flight" in the Twin Otter.

Acknowledgements

In composing these daily communications from Paul MacVittie to his son, there are many who have contributed inspiration, encouragement and life stories. These are too numerous to list— their influence is quoted throughout these "Thoughts for Today." The author's wife, Robbin, has been his "wing-woman" in saving, editing and sending out these daily messages. Special people have pushed for publication (Fred Waldman, at heart another son to the author; Priscilla McDonnell, "the world's Best Mother-in-Law"; and many others who have enjoyed receiving copies over the years). We want to particularly thank Martha Carlson Bradley who, as our initial editor, helped bring some order and direction to the immense volume of material, and Jasmine Lai who documented sources for numerous quotes and Annette Horn, Lauren Packnick (Prose and Commas Editorial), Adam Thomas, and especially Red Sanchez who have helped bring it to its final form. We are also grateful to Thomas G Wilson for his generosity in sharing his photography of Mac as a pilot in action. But, of course, the motivation for these daily thoughts is the author's son, Mac.

References

Astronaut-Senator John Glenn dies at 95; draws plaudits. (2016, December 8). *Salina Journal*. Retrieved from https://www.salina.com/6ae93a91-2c98-5b7d-9a35-354c7df75a35.html?template=ampart

Augustine. (1943). *Confessions*. (F. Sheed, Trans.) London: Sheed and Ward.

Bonar, A. (n.d.). *www.goodreads.com*. Retrieved April 23, 2020, from www.goddreads.com: https://www.goodreads. com/quotes/541963-let-us-be-as-watchful-after-the-victory-as-before

Born, M. (2005). The Born - Einstein Letters 1916-1955: Friendship, Politics, and Physics in Uncertain Times. New York: Macmillan. Retrieved from Physics Today.

Breathnach, S. B. (1996). *Simple Abundance Journal of Gratitude*, The. New York: Grand Central Publishing.

Brooks, E. S. (1898). *The True Story of Benjamin Franklin, the American Statesman*. Boston: Lothrop Publishing Co.

Bruschi, T. (2009, August 31). Tedy Bruschi Press Conference. (R. Kraft, Interviewer) Retrieved from https://www.patriots.com/news/tedy-bruschi-press-conference-160781

Bryan, W. J. (1899). Retrieved from http://trisagionseraph. tripod. com/Texts/America.html

Burns, R. (1787). "To a Louse, On Seeing One on a Lady's Bonnet at Church". *Poems, Chiefly in the Scottish Dialect*. Edinburgh: William Creech.

Burrowes, T. (n.d.). *Pennsylvania School Journal*. Lancaster: Wm. B. Wiley.

Carman, B. (1904). *The World's Best Poetry*. (B. e. Carman, Ed.) Philadelphia: John D. Morris & Co.

Chandler, J. (2009, August 31). *Belichick, Bruschi Forever Linked with Patriots*. Retrieved from New England Sports News: https://nesn.com/2009/08/belichick-bruschi-forev-er-linked/

Churchill, W. (1940, January 20). *National Churchill Museum*. Retrieved from Winston Churchill/Speeches/19040 Speeches/A House of Many Mansions: https://www.national-churchillmuseum.org/a-house-of-many-mansions.html.

Cicero. (n.d.). *Epistulae ad Familiares*. Retrieved from Latin Library: https://www.thelatinlibrary.com/cicero/fam9.shtml

Clark, D. (n.d.). *Surrender Your Key to the Kingdom Within*. Bloomington: iUniverse, Inc.

Clay, C. (2011, February). *Muhammad Ali – Pre Liston Poetry & Highlights*. Retrieved from YouTube: https://www.youtube. com/watch?v=JwPPM_vaNrI

Coue, E. (1922). *Self Mastery Through Conscious Autosuggestions*. New York: Malkan Pub. Co.

Cowper, W. (1773). Light Shining Out of Darkness. (C. W. Shapiro, Ed.) *The Columbia Anthology of British Poetry.*

Eckhart, M. (1924). *Meister Eckhart* (Vol. 2). (F. Pfeiffer, Ed., & C. d. Evans, Trans.) J.M. Watkins.

Edison, T. A. (n.d.). *AZQuotes.com.* Retrieved April 23, 2020, from AZQuotes.com: https://www.azquotes.com/quote/906005

Eisenhower, D. D. (1956). *Dwight D. Eisenhower Presidential Library, Museum & Boyhood Home.* Retrieved from National Archives: https://www.eisenhowerlibrary.gov/eisenhowers/quotes#Citizenship

Elliot, J. (1978). *The Journals of Jim Elliot.* (E. Elliot, Ed.) Grand Rapids: Revell.

Emerson, R. W. (1874). *Essays, First Series.* Boston: James R. Osgood & Co.

Emerson, R. W. (1909). *Essays and English Traits* (Vol. 5). (C.

W. Eliot, Ed.) New York City: P.F. Collier & Son. Retrieved from www.bartleby.com

Emerson, R. W. (n.d.). *Essays and Lectures.* New York: Literary Classics of the United States, Inc.

Emerson, R. W., & Ed. Atkinson, B. (1940). *"Spiritual Laws." (The Complete Essays and other Writings of Ralph Waldo Emerson.).* New York: Random House.

Frankl, V. E. (1959). *Man's Search for Meaning.* New York: Simon & Schuster.

Frankl, V. E. (1986). *The Doctor and the Soul*. Visalia: Vintage Press.

Fromm, E. (1976). *To Have or to Be?* New York City: Harper & Row.

Gardner, J. W. (1961). *Excellence: Can We Be Equal and Excellent Too?* New York: W. W. Norton.

Gilbert, J. H. (1895). *Dictionary of Burning Words of Brilliant Writers*. New York: W. B. Ketcham.

Hagopian Institute. (2008). *Quote Junkie: Greek and Roman Edition: An Interesting Collection of Quotes from the Greatest Greek and Roman Philosophers and Leaders*. CreateSpace Publishing.

Hupfeld, H. (1931). *As Time Goes By*. New York.

Hyken, S. (2016, February 27). There's No Traffic Jam On The Extra Mile. *Forbes*. Retrieved from https://www.forbes.com/ sites/ shephyken/2016/02/27/theres-no-traffic-jam-on-the-ex- tra-mile/#7672fbb279a6

Keller, H. (1903). *Optimism, An Essay*. Boston: D.B. Updike, The Merrymount Press.

Kierkegaard, S. (n.d.). *www.quotepark.com*. Retrieved April 23, 2020, from www.quotepark.com: https://quotepark.com/ quotes/691569-soren-kierkegaard-life-can-only-be-under-stood-backwards-but-it-must/

Kubler-Ross, E. (2003). *Kubler-Ross, Elisabeth.* Retrieved from Wikiquote: https://en.wikiquote.org/wiki/Elisabeth_Kübler-Ross

Leone, S. (Director). (1966). *The Good, the Bad, and the Ugly* [Motion Picture].

Longstaff, W. D. (ca. 1882). Take Time to be Holy.

Lounsbury, T. R. (1912). *Yale Book of American Verse.* New Haven: Yale University Press.

Magee Jr., J. G. (2009, May 18). *Arlington National Cemetery. Where Valor Proudly Sleeps.* Retrieved April 09, 2020, from High Flight: http://www.arlingtoncemetery.net/highflig.htm

Marden, O. (1903). *The Young Man Entering Business.* T. Y. Crowell.

Maslow, A. H. (1994). *Religions, Values, and Peak Experiences.* New York: Penguin. Retrieved from https://www.academia.edu/37619593/Religions_Values_and_Peak_Experiences_Abraham_H._Maslow

Maxwell, J. C. (2007). *Talent Is Never Enough.* Nashville. Nelson Business.

Maxwell, J. C. (2007). *Beyond Talent: Become Someone Who Gets Extraordinary Results.* Nashville: Thomas Nelson.

May, R. (1981). *Freedom and Destiny.* New York: W.W. Norton & Co.

McCain, J., & Salter, M. (1999). *Faith of My Fathers: A Memoir.* New York City: Penguin Random House LLC.

McLaughlin, K. (1945, December 22). Gen. Patton Dies Quietly in Sleep; Burial in Europe. *New York Times, Vol. XCV. No. 32,109.* New York.

Mead, G. R. (1901). *Apollonius of Tyana, The Philosopher-Reformer of the First Century A.D.* London: Theosophical Publishing Society.

Mill, J. S. (1862, February). The Contest in America. *Fraser's Magazine.* Retrieved from Amost Chosen People. A Blog about American History, and the Development of a Great Nation.

Moore, G. F. (1922). *History of Religions* (Vol. 1).

Mother Theresa Quotes. (n.d.). Retrieved from Quotes.net: www. quotes.net/quote/42607

Nietzsche, F. (1911). *The Twilight of the Idols.* Edinburgh: T.N. Foulis.

Parent, J. (2002). *www.audible.com.* Retrieved from www. audible. com: https://www.audible.com/pd/You-Cant-Stop-the- Waves-But-You-Can-Learn-to-Surf-Audiobook/B01MSK28TW

Patton, G. S. (1944, December 14). *History on the Net.* Retrieved April 23, 2020, from History on the Net: https://www. historyonthenet.com/when-patton-enlisted-the-entire-third-army-to-pray-for-fair-weather

Peale, N. V. (1974). *You Can If You Think You Can*. New York: Fireside.

Peterson, W. A. (1972). *The Art of Living, Day by Day: Three Hundred and Sixty-five Thoughts, Ideas, Ideals, Experiences, Adventures, Inspirations, to Enrich Your Life*. New York: Simon and Schuster.

Piper, W. (2005). *The Little Engine That Could*. London: Penguin Group.

Plutarch. (1898). *Morals [Plutarch's Morals: Ethical Essays, Shilleto trans.]*. London: George Bell and Sons.

Riesman, D. (2000). In D. L. Merton, Social Science Quotations: *Who Said What, When, and Where*. New Brunswick: Transaction Publishers.

Roosevelt, T. (1917, Jan 26). *Letter from Theodore Roosevelt to the Congress of Constructive Patriotism held under the auspices of the National Security League, Washington, D.C., January 26, 1917. Printed letter to S. Stanwood Menken, Esq., Chairman, Committee on Congress of Construct*. Retrieved April 09, 2020,

from Theodore Roosevelt Center at Dickinson State University: https://www.theodorerooseveltcenter.org/Research/Digi-tal-Library/Record?libID=o283065

Rose, N. (2016, May 28). *Honoring the Forefathers: Abraham Maslow and the Quest for Self-Actualization*. Retrieved from Mappalicious: The German Side of Positive Psychology: https://mappalicious.com/2016/05/28/honoring-the-forefa-thers-abraham-maslow-and-the-quest-for-self-actualization/

Rosenthal, R. J. (1968). Pygmalion in the classroom. *In Urban Rev 3* (pp. 16-20). Retrieved from https://doi.org/10.1007/BF02322211

Rotella, Bob, & Cullen, Bob. (2004). *The Golfer's Mind: Play to be Great*. New York: Free Press.

Russell, B., & Branch, T. (1979). *Second Wind: The Memories of an Opinionated Man*. New York: Random House.

Salzgeber, N. (2017). *35 Timeless Life Lessons & Quotes From John Wooden, The Greatest Coach Ever*. Retrieved from NJ Life Hacks: https://www.njlifehacks.com/john-wooden-quotes-les-sons/

Schelling, F. W. (1809). *Philosophische Untersuchungen* über *das Wesen der Menschlichen Freiheit [Of Human Freedom]*.

Schonberg, C.-M., Boublil, A., Natel, J. -M & Kretzmer, H. (2009). I Dreamed a Dream [Recorded by S. Boyle]. On *I Dreamed a Dream*. S. Mac.

Schonberg, C.-M., Boublil, A., Natel, J.-M., & Kretzmer, H. (1985). Les Miserables [Recorded by O. L. Cast]. London: C. Mackintosh, producer.

Schweitzer, A. (1947). *Albert Schweitzer: An Anthology*. (C. R. Joy, Ed.) Boston: The Beacon Press.

Shakespeare, W. (1604). Measure for Measure (Act 1, Scene iv).

Shakespeare, W. (1623). Julius Caesar (Act I, scene ii).
Shakespeare, W. (1605). Hamlet (Act 5, Scene ii).

Shaw, G. B. (1961). *Too True to Be Good*. New York: Samuel French.

Sherman, J. (1992). *A Sampler of Jewish-American Folklore*. Little Rock: August House Publishing.

Simpson, J., & Speake, J. (2008). *Oxford Dictionary of Proverbs, The*. Oxford: Oxford University Press.

Snow, T. (2007, May 12). Commencement Address at Catholoc University of America. Washington D.C. Retrieved from http://publicaffairs.cua.edu/Releases/2007//07CommencementAddress.cfm

Spielberg, S. (Director). (1989). *Indiana Jones and the Last Crusade* [Motion Picture].

Twain, M. (1902). *www.twainquotes.com*. Retrieved April 23, 2020, from www.twainquotes.com: http://www.twainquotes.com/Pessimism.html

Wesley, C., Whitefield, G., & Mendelssohn, F. (1739). Hark! The Herald Angels Sing. *Hymns and Sacred Poems*.

Whitman, W. (1892). *Prose Works*. Philadelphia: David McK-ay.

Whittier, J. G. (1912). Maud Muller. *Yale Book of American Verse*. (T. R. Lounsbury, Ed.) New Haven, Connecticut: Yale University Press.

Wirt, W. (1973). Sketches of the Life and Character of Patrick Henry. In L. Copeland, & L. W. Lamm, *The World's Great Speeches*. New York: Dover Publications.

Wooden, J., & Jamison, S. (2007). *The Essential Wooden: A Lifetime of Lessons on Leaders and Leadership*. McGraw-Hill Education.

CPSIA information can be obtained
at www.ICGtesting.com
Printed in the USA
LVHW081610221122
733802LV00016B/1005